Northumberland: the Coast

A journey through the coastline of Northumberland

Stephen Wood

With photography by the people of Northumbria

Orwell House

for my parents

who taught me the value of the Northumbrian Coast

Contents

Cover photo: Anne Nicholson

© Ordnance Survey OpenData

ONE

THIS GREAT KINGDOM, NORTHUMBERLAND

Northumberland: the northernmost county in England, the least densely populated, uniquely dramatic, and steeped in history. County Durham lies to the south, Cumbria to the west, and the border with Scotland to the north. To the east there is only the sea, calm and sparkling or mountainous grey depending on its mood. The coastline stretches over 60 miles as the crow flies from the mouth of the river Tyne to a few miles north of Berwick on Tweed. It's a beautiful coast - sweeping bays of sand and dunes, rocky promontories, old stone harbours and wide skies, home to crying seabirds, the smell of salt, ozone and the sweet tang of the tide.

The boundaries of Northumberland have moved around over the centuries, but for many years the river Tyne defined its southern border. Then, in the 1970s, that boundary was redefined to accommodate the new Metropolitan Borough of North Tyneside, pushing the county line a few miles north to Seaton Sluice. But for me, born and bred here more than 67 years ago, and for many like me, this land on the north bank of the Tyne is still Northumberland.

I'm standing on the headland overlooking the river, a breeze cooling the warmth of the July sunshine. The north pier stretches out, straight as a die, almost a kilometre into the North Sea, the pinnacle of its lighthouse at the end. Across the wide water of the estuary lies the county of Durham, Land of the Prince Bishops, Catherine Cookson, the Angel of the North and the Great North Road. A fishing boat bound for the fish quay at North Shields butts upriver into the tide, surrounded by shrieking gulls. At the foot of the pier is the small crescent of sand and rocks known as Prior's Haven with the tinkling rigging and pennants of the Sailing Club. Close by stands the lofty column of Collingwood's Monument, memorial to Nelson's second-in-command, watching over the river with regal authority. Behind and above me are the ruins of the castle and the priory, legacies of a deep and ancient history. This is the beginning of my Northumberland.

From here my journey is northwards, up the coast through the Victorian playground of Whitley Bay, on through industrial Blyth past Newbiggin and Cresswell into the wilder country that begins at Druridge Bay. Past Amble where the coastline grows increasingly remote, paths wander through the dunes and figures on the beaches become ever-more solitary. The villages of Alnmouth, Boulmer, Craster, Embleton and Low Newton speckle the shoreline, and on through Beadnell and Seahouses to Bamburgh. From there the wide sands and flats of Lindisfarne give onto a coastline of immense cultural and religious heritage, meeting Goswick Sands, Cheswick beach and Spittal at the fore of Berwick with its great walls. A few miles beyond lies the border with Scotland. 64 continuous kilometres of this coast, between the estuary of the river Coquet at Amble and Berwick-on-Tweed, are designated an Area of Outstanding Natural Beauty. This is indeed a grand land.

For me the persisting image of the Northumbrian coast is a solitary walker sauntering on a wide expanse of sand, firm beneath his feet from the outgoing tide. His dog bounds on the shoreline. He clutches his coat about him and leans forward as the dunes bend and sway in the wind. A slate sky stretches out above a white flecked grey sea. Gulls cry overhead, wheeling like kites. But different seasons bring different pictures, and here on the far north east coast sometimes the seasons conspire and compete with each other in the course of a single day. It's a land of constant change and for every observer there is a different perspective, a uniquely personal story.

The power of the North Sea upon the north pier at Tynemouth, for me the southern boundary of Northumberland

Photo: John Fatkin

There are, of course, other coastlines available. I recently heard Rick Stein on television extolling the virtues of the Cornish coast with its prehistoric cliffs, quaint coves and steeply tumbling villages. He spoke passionately about the light as I recall. And Norfolk has beaches of such scale that they have been used as locations in films like Shakespeare in Love, The Eagle Has Landed and many others. There's the magnificent drama of the Scottish coast, and North Yorkshire too. I could go on. In fact, it's impossible to identify a seaboard county in the whole of the United Kingdom that doesn't proclaim its coastline in one way or another. So why Northumberland? Well, I would mention the light, in spite of what Rick Stein had to say about Cornwall. The sun rises over the sea in the east, so often in spectacular colour. I would speak of its sweeping bays, its rocky promontories, secret coves, majestic castles and the soft pastels of the sands and the dune grasses. But more than anything I would tell of its space. On an overcrowded island it's hard to imagine a place where two miles of coastline can be quite so deserted, or perhaps occupied only by that distant solitary figure and a dog. Even in high season when the natural beauty of the area attracts visitors and tourists from afar, it remains a place of peace where the silence is broken only by the sounds of nature, the sea, the wind, and the seabirds crying overhead. The peace and space, that's why.

This is not a history book, but the history that forged this coastline will inevitably mark our journey. It's a place where the trades of the sea, shipwrecks and smuggling litter the pages of its bygone years. The great castles of Dunstanburgh and Bamburgh both witnessed battle and siege in the Wars of the Roses. King Oswald, Saint Bede and Saint Cuthbert, to name but three famous incumbents, all left their marks here, as did Henry Hotspur, Capability Brown, George Stephenson, the great industrialist William Armstrong, and the great houses of the Percys, the Dukes of Northumberland. History rises from the ancient ruins of the priories of Lindisfarne and here at Tynemouth, below which I stand now, and the less obvious, the less celebrated features of this coast which speak to us of its ancestry – ancient fingers of rock stretching out into the waves, older by millennia than anything put here by the hand of man. Even the defences of the 2nd world war lying abandoned in the sands and among the shoreline dunes have their place.

Sunrise over the Tyne estuary and the masts of the sailing club in Prior's Haven

Photo: Helen Cowan

3

This is my personal journey along the coastline of Northumberland, but I have with me its people, the common denominator that binds it all together. From the Geordies of Tyneside to the men of the borders, Northumbrians all, they are the people who live here, who make their livings here and awake to its splendour every morning. They defend its heritage and curate its landscape. From the institutions of the National Trust and English Heritage to the independent pubs and businesses, and from the smallest shoreline cottage to the great bastion of Bamburgh Castle, there is a staunch sense of belonging held by anyone who has found their connection to these lands.

And so who more fitting than they to illustrate this journey for us? Those who are passionate about their county, some with little more than a phone wandering the beach with their dog, others up before the dawn with bags and lenses, filters and tripods, professionals and amateurs and some in-between. They have, all of them, captured their landscape in their uniquely individual ways, for their own reasons and with their own personal stories behind each picture.

Before I leave the mouth of the river and point myself northwards, the words of Robson Green come to mind:

"But it's in the land that I belong
In its castles, hills and sand,
Forever will abide with me
This Great Kingdom, Northumberland."

TWO

TYNEMOUTH & WHITLEY BAY

Before taking my first footsteps north I ambled around the headland for a while. I met a young lady who was gazing out into the estuary through binoculars. She was dolphin watching and turned out to be something of an expert, a member of the Cetacean Society. She told me that she knew all the animals by name, but I have no idea if that was true or if she just identified me as someone who would fall for that sort of thing. But dolphins are a frequent sight on this coast, and I'm likely to see several more, or perhaps more of the same one, in the course of the next few days.

From the root of the pier I walked up the small road that winds steeply for 300 yards or so to the flat apron at the end of Tynemouth Front Street where an ornate little clock tower stands in the middle of a wide, flagged area and the road turns north up the coast. There are new apartments here, the Gibraltar Rock pub, and across the dry, green moat is the entrance to the castle and the priory on the headland.

The entrance to Tynemouth Castle & Priory, from the end of Front Street

Photo: the author

This is only a stone's throw from the industries of the river. Not so many years ago it was shipbuilding with all its noise, oil and smoke. Shipyards clattered with the sound of riveters and welders, cheek by jowl with tight rows of poor terraced housing. Most of that has gone now, replaced by the constructions of modern living. The remnants of a fishing industry hangs on at North Shields, and the bonded warehouses and container gantries of the Port of Tyne across the water on the Durham side pierce the skyline, but it's mostly the domain of new apartment complexes, boutique bars and restaurants, and in places the cleared, fenced-off concrete bases on which more will be constructed. But even back in the dirty days, ever since the early Victorians made it accessible by train, here in Tynemouth and next-door Whitley Bay the coast attracted visitors away from all that toil to the sands and entertainments. In those days the Northern Riviera, as this part of the coast has been known, thronged with tourists enjoying the beaches, ice-creams, the salt-water pools and a host of family, and not so family, entertainment.

When the shipbuilding industry collapsed in the recession of the 1970s and 1980s, along with its close relative coalmining, local economies struggled, hotels fell into disrepair and amenities declined. But in recent years, as injections of cash and optimism have changed (and raised) the game on the riverside, the coast has followed suit and here at the end of the broad Front Street there is an air of calm affluence. The shops, boutiques and cafes are appealing, clean and cared for, the grass around the castle and priory entrance is groomed and mown, and The Gibraltar Rock has a welcoming face.

Only a few paces north from the end of Front Street the road winds above the sandy, seaweed crescent of King Edward's Bay, squeezed between high cliffs with a steeply zig-zagging, knee-grinding path leading down to the shore. There's a little shack down there from which seafood and beer are to be had amidst clouds of smoke. It's popular, and summer evenings glimmer with the lights of outdoor tables and the fires of beach barbeques on the sands. This bay is popular with surfers too, and as I gazed down from the cliff-top I could see their black rubber-suited figures bobbing about in the waves offshore. Behind me and overlooking the sea is the refined crescent of Percy Gardens, an arc of affluent, Victorian 4 storey terraces which have arguably the best views of this coastline for miles around.

Round the headland above King Edward's Bay the coastline north comes into view. The broad arc of sand known as Longsands curves away to the distant spire of St George's Church and the headland that protects the little harbour cove at Cullercoats. The beach here is popular, as it was in years gone by. In the mid to late 19th century before the age of the motor car, the Longsands thronged with the style of the time - wooden bathing machines wheeled up to the water's edge, waxed moustaches and striped one-piece costumes for the men, and full dresses, long pantaloons tied at the knee and frilly bathing caps for the ladies. In fact, those joyous days rolled on after Victoria passed the throne to Edward VII, on to George V, briefly to Edward VIII, George VI and finally to our present queen Elizabeth II. Styles and society's conventions changed over those periods, and two world wars came and went, but Tynemouth and Whitley Bay always retained their identities as destinations for the seaside holidaymakers of those times.

There was much to draw them here. Halfway along the arc of The Longsands, towering over the beach, was The Plaza, a huge Victorian pleasuredome built in 1878 and which, in its day, hosted ballrooms, an ice-rink, night-clubs, restaurants and bars. And set into the base of the cliff below where I am standing, The Lido, or Tynemouth Outdoor Pool as it is also known. Built in 1925, it's a rectangular, concrete

King Edward's Bay below the promontory at Tynemouth and the ruins of the castle and the priory
Photo: Dawn Roberts

salt water pool set into the rocks against the sandy beach. It used to be bright, white and blue, with tiered concrete seating. Beauty contests were held there, amateur swimming contests and knobbly knees competitions. I remember coming here as a child with my parents. It epitomised the attractions of this Northern Riviera - carefree leisure.

But when the 1970s brought shipyard redundancies and cheap package holidays to Benidorm the Lido's customers stayed away, and with disuse the pool decayed. Over time the concrete greyed and crumbled, the paint on the ironwork of the railings peeled and rusted into streaky brown. As I looked down upon it today it's an eyesore, half full of sand, and in spite of tentative enthusiasm from local groups there is little evidence that it will be restored.

The modern age abandoned The Plaza too. Under-used and poorly maintained, in the 1970s it went into a steady downhill decline. It became seedy and down-at-heel, and as the queues lengthened at the Jobcentres so the great building found itself also unemployed. In 1996 it suspiciously caught fire and the resulting remains were bulldozed out of the way. There remains nothing of it now, just the dunes and sands running down to the shore.

The Plaza, The Lido and other features like them, the Victoriana and the Art Deco inspired flapper styles of the inter-war years have mostly gone. But 21st century Tynemouth offers much for the modern visitor. Now the features of this coast's Victorian heritage are subsumed by a new landscape, and the entertainment provided by the likes of The Plaza has been replaced by high end cafes offering espressos and seafood, small independent outlets to service the needs of surfers, bathers, windsurfers, joggers and those just relaxing on the sands. The Grand Hotel overlooking the sea-front, as up and down in fortune as The Plaza over the years, is now plush and resplendent, as its Victorian founders intended it to be.

Longsands today is a wide beach with grassy dunes through which little paths and tracks lead down to the sands. There are no parades of shops here, no amusement arcades or fun fairs, only the beach, the boating lake and its little park with rose gardens, bowling greens and tennis courts. The low, modernist architecture of the Tynemouth Aquarium sits next to the art deco Park Hotel with its white balconies and rounded, nautical lines, only a few hundred yards from my childhood home. It's a pleasant walk along the sands, or along the promenade or the paths above it. Beyond the green space above the beach where years ago Billy Smart erected his circus big top, the steeple of St George's church marks the end of the bay.

Above: *Tynemouth Longsands looking north towards St George's Church and Cullercoats*

Below: *Longsands looking south towards Tynemouth headland and the north pier*

Photos: Gren Sowerby

The promontory at the northern end of Tynemouth Longsands guards Cullercoats where stubby piers enclose the little bay with its lifeboat station, colourful fishing boats hauled up above the tideline, and the highly regarded Marine Laboratory where the University of Newcastle's School of Marine Science conducts its experiments and research. There are old smugglers' caves here where I played as a child with my little pals, shooting each other with machine guns of driftwood. I remember the caves were dank and smelly then, places where local romantics might steal a kiss or more from a willing lass, and teenage ruffians would drink from bottles, smoke, set off fireworks or simply urinate. Today the caves are clean, free of litter and smelling only of the sea. Above the cliff a small parade of seaside shops and cafes provide a place to sit and gaze over the harbour to the expanse of the North Sea, where container ships, ferries and occasionally cruise liners lie at anchor awaiting permission or tide to enter the Tyne.

Cullercoats Bay   *Photo: Dawn Roberts*

Past Cullercoats and the rocky fingers of Brown's Bay the approach to Whitley Bay is a wide promenade lined by guest houses, private hotels and cafes. There are more surfers here, beach cafes and good, soft sand on which to lay a towel or a deckchair. The location of a coffee, or a beer or two, is never far away. But this is not Blackpool, or Brighton. There is no rollercoaster dominating the skyline, and there are fewer shops selling the tasteless tat that passes for souvenirs, though I daresay you could find a tee-shirt with *"I Love Whitley Bay"* on it if you look hard enough.

The focal point of the Whitley Bay seafront is The Spanish City, so called because of its Iberian architecture. Its white dome is singularly the notable feature of the Whitley Bay skyline. Built in 1910 as a concert hall and tearoom, over the years it has housed a variety of entertainments and within its acre of land a permanent funfair with a helter-skelter, dodgems, rifle ranges and coconut shies. Like so many other places it suffered badly in the 1970s and 1980s, but today it's undergone a remarkable transformation and is now an elegant centre for dining, shopping and relaxing with a drink. There are boutique retail outlets and brass framed menus at the entrance doors. It's a wedding venue and a conference centre, and I stopped to take a coffee in its elegant champagne bar. The views out over the sea, the links and the pinnacle of St Mary's Island lighthouse in the distance are exceptional.

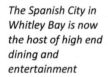

The Spanish City in Whitley Bay is now the host of high end dining and entertainment

Photo: Helen Cowan

The walk along the coast from the Spanish City, north from the town, is wide and open. Broad green links separate the promenade from the coast road. It's a mile or so of pleasant amble down those links with panoramic views out to sea, past the pleasant Victorian café set into the promenade and the pitch & putt course which has been there since I was a child. The green, wooden hut from which clubs and balls are available looks to be exactly the same, 60 years later. Then Whitley Bay abruptly ends. The coast road takes an elbow inland for a few hundred yards to avoid a static caravan park and the farmland that borders the coast here, and a narrow road leads a few hundred yards down to St Mary's Island and its towering, white lighthouse.

Stunning images of St Mary's Island

*Photo **right:** Ant Clark, and **below** Helen Cowan*

One of the most photographed locations on this part of the coast, St Mary's Island marks the northern end of the "Northern Riviera", as this part of the coast has been known. The lighthouse was fully operational until 1984 when modern technology replaced it. It is still maintained as a visitor centre

Photo: Gren Sowerby

Formally known as Bait Island, St Mary's is a tidal island, cut off from the mainland twice a day and accessible, when the tide permits, by a concrete causeway. The headland here is known as Curry's Point, after Michael Curry who was hanged here in 1739 for the murder of the landlord of a local pub. Standing on the spot where the gibbet was erected, I wonder what the landlord had done, or served, to invoke such reprisal from Mr Curry.

There has been a settlement of one sort or another on the island for many centuries – monks, smugglers, and even the Romans had a presence here. In the mid-18th century some more substantial buildings were erected, small dwellings and even an inn. It must have been a dark, remote coastline in those days and the pub, now long gone, had a chequered history of smuggling and dark deeds. The lighthouse itself was built in 1898. It was switched off in 1984 when modern navigation technology replaced it, and has since been maintained by North Tyneside Council as a visitor centre where today there is a gift shop, video presentations and the opportunity to climb the 137 steps to the top which I declined in view of my appalling head for heights, but it's a peaceful place to potter about the rocks and pools.

From the island shore where the surf gurgles about the rocks and holes I stood for a while and took in the view back south, the sum of my journey so far, all the way back past the bays and promontories to the line of Tynemouth pier striking out to sea in the distance. There are a lot of memories for me here, this playground of my childhood. I can easily summon the images – the outdoor pool in summer with my parents and brother, crisps and fizzy pop, the tang of salt water in my mouth; the Rex hotel, a venue for rock bands and under-age brown ale; the boating lake with its minnows, sticklebacks and model yachts; the Plaza, the Spanish City, amusement arcades and pinball machines, and many others.

This is the place to which my father brought my mother in 1950, to escape the mines of County Durham. Here he forged his career on Tyneside in the business of ships, raised his family, and made me a Geordie. His ashes are scattered in the cemetery just over the road from St Mary's Island.

Above - An iconic view of the Spanish City – photo: Dawn Roberts

Right – Sunrise over St Mary's Island – photo: Helen Cowan

THREE

ST MARY'S ISLAND TO BLYTH

From St Mary's island the main road loops inland for a few hundred yards to avoid the caravan park and then north through a stretch of farmland. Just before the Delaval Arms is the road-sign which welcomes travellers to Northumberland.

The coastal path wanders along the cliffs above a couple of rocky coves and patches of sand. High cliffs don't feature much on the generally low coastline of Northumbria other than back at Tynemouth, at the border when I get there, and here beneath the small community of Hartley where paths lead down to the shore. There's a sea wall and a small promenade here, overlooking the shingle and rock slabs of Collywell Bay. A few yards offshore there's a stubby rock formation known intriguingly as *"Charlie's Garden"*. It's said that in the 19th century a local gentleman called Charles Dockwray cultivated the top of this sandstone pinnacle before natural erosion separated it from the mainland. It's a good story and appeals to anyone with a sense of the absurd. Charlie Dockwray must have been delightfully eccentric, pottering about with his spuds and dahlias on the top of a rock amidst the surf and waves of the North Sea. But there's little compelling evidence that there's much truth in the tale. The reports that I have read are usually qualified by words like *"reputedly"* and *"supposedly"*, so perhaps the legend of Charlie Dockwray was born more in the local hostelries than in actual fact. But who knows?

Charlie's Garden in Colywell Bay, said to have been once connected to the mainland

Photo: Derek Taylor

Right: Charlie's Garden – Photo Derek Taylor

Below: Seaton Sluice – Photo: Nathan Atkinson

Immediately beyond Collywell Bay is Seaton Sluice. It's a name that suggests something uncomfortably effluent and certainly charmless. This is far from the truth and crossing over the Seaton Burn and the sluice from which the place takes its name it is, in fact, rather lovely and quaint.

The hand of man and the natural emergence of the burn have together created a unique configuration of inlet, harbour and grassy dune. Where the Seaton Burn met the sea was a small, natural harbour. It was prone to silting up and in the mid-17th century sluice gates were installed allowing tidal surges to scour the channel and flush the sand and silt away out to sea. Later in the 1760s the harbour entrance was improved by blasting a cutting through the rock creating what is now known as "*The Cut*", or locally and more prosaically "*The Gut*", a narrow entrance to the small harbour itself where now blue and white boats are moored, leaning onto the mud at low tide.

Around the narrow inlet from the sea are green banks and dunes. In days long ago salt exporting and glass-making were carried on here. There was once a huge bottle factory which engaged labour from miles around and so extensive was the industry of this place that the works incorporated a market, a brewery, a granary, a brickyard and six tall conical brick furnaces. All that's all gone now. What is

left is a grassy headland backwater, the sluice itself with small boats occupying the moorings, the Waterford Arms which was once offices of some sort for the glass industry, and The Kings Arms pub standing alone on the headland nursing a history bound with tales of dark mischief.

It's a grassy, pleasant place to sit and watch the quietness of the coast, relaxing on the green around the harbour. I arranged to meet one of our local photographers here, Ant Clark, but by the time I arrived outside the Kings Arms it had come on to rain, and I thought it would be safer to go inside. It's a pub with a fine reputation and we spent a pleasant pint discussing Ant's

work and his love of this coast. He's a proper photographer with loads of experience in high-level commercial photography, and he has a camera that probably cost more than my car, so once back outside when the rain had eased off it would have been churlish to deny him the opportunity of taking my picture outside the pub.

Ant left me there, probably suspicious that I would try to find another pub, so I pressed on alone towards Blyth.

It would have been churlish.... Photo: Ant Clark

North beyond Seaton Sluice Cut a long sandy crescent arcs into the distance towards Blyth. This is the long, flat and wide expanse of sand that is Hartley Links, becoming Blyth South Beach as it nears the town. The road runs for about 2 miles close to the coast, separated from the sands by the wide, low humps and hillocks of grassy dunes, and inland to the west the open aspect of low farmland. There are numerous parking laybys for the many who walk and seek their leisure on the sands here. Like so many beaches I will encounter on this journey it's open to all the elements of the sea and has a feeling of great vastness which belies the urban outreaches of Tyneside which straggle along the coast here behind the coastal dunes and the road. Its low, flat sands, dark brown and firm from the tide, reach into softer sands and the low grasses and dunes that hide the road and the urbanity beyond. But the signs of habitation and commercial enterprise are not far away. The silos and cranes of Blyth mark the end of the sands against the spindly, wooden framework of the south pier.

Where the sands end at Blyth there are light industrial units, the harbour offices and the Royal Northumberland Yacht Club, and also a wide promenade with artistic tiling, an information centre, toilets (not to be sniffed at on the Northumbrian coast - they can be few and far between), and a small enclave of retail outlets offering fish and chips, coffees and ice cream. Above a colourful row of beach huts a restored World War II gun emplacement purposely directs its long, grey barrels out to sea.

I accosted a stout gentleman who seemed to be at a loose end, sitting alone on a bench. I asked him for some information about this place and he turned out to be the owner of one of the gift shops and the lifeguard tower above it. He told me that there are plans for more development here, one of the major takeaway outlets, more shopping, a new pub and the infrastructure of the 21st century. I hope they don't go and spoil it.

Right: *Blyth Beach, northwards from Seaton Sluice Photo: Dawn Roberts*

Below left: *Colourful beach huts at Blyth Photo: Nathan Atkinson*

Below Right: *Blyth south pier Photo: Paul Turner*

From here by the south pier there is no crossing over the river Blyth until up through the town to the bridge that carries the main road. It's a working port with all the associated metal, machinery and rather messy light industry. There is no public access to much of the waterfront where the quay is lined with light wharves and industrial units, and even the England Coast Path has to take a long detour away from the coast here to avoid it. I passed an area where massive cable spools, at least 20 feet and more in diameter, were laid out along the roadside. Eventually, the road leads back down to the quayside and my base for this section of my journey, The Commissioner's Quay Inn.

The Commissioner's Quay Inn, Blyth   Photo: The Inn Collection Group

In my childhood Blyth was synonymous with oily industry and to a large extent deprivation. Today, the quayside is modern and cleaner than I expected. A massive rig-support vessel (described as *"Boaty McBoatface"* by a follower of the blog I was writing each evening on the journey, and I could see the likeness) was tied up on the opposite side of the river beneath 3 towering silos and gantries. After dinner as the light was fading into dusk I ventured out into the calm evening air. The rain had stopped and a slight reddening appeared in the sky.

The lights of shipping and industry came on, and in the half-light there was a little romance amidst the quiet industry of Blyth. The air was dead still yet the blades of the massive wind turbine that overshadows the quayside were still turning. How was that? It was stirring stuff, a tonic for the soul.

Blyth Quayside   *Photo: the author*

FOUR

BLYTH TO CRESSWELL

Looking from the Commissioner's Quay Inn, over the river where the big ship was tied up against the silos and gantries, it's actually a long tongue of land, a narrow spit formed between the coast and the river Blyth that runs just inland for almost 2 miles before it ends at the long north pier and the sea. Here there is a rather ramshackle, industrial landscape, a long stretch of sand, the small settlement of Cambois, the estuary of the river Wansbeck, and then the town of Newbiggin-on-Sea.

Because of all that fenced and guarded industry the beach below the silos is hard to get to and in any case it's not a place I thought was likely to offer much in the way of pleasant aspect. But my mission was to see all of this coastline and the day was fine enough so I drove up through Blyth, across the main road bridge, and then back down tortuous small lanes towards the coast on the other side. I drove amidst alternately pleasant rural fields, woodland and swathes of industrial wasteland then down the spit of land between the river and the sea on a narrow track. Eventually I discovered the security gates and the end of public access in front of the silos I had seen from the other side of the river.

I didn't feel like troubling the people in high visibility jackets and hard hats by asking if it would be alright to wander about with my camera, so I retreated back north towards Cambois seeking a place to park and discover this beach. An old rusty, weedy railway line runs beside the road.

Cambois seems oddly Gallic for a Northumbrian place-name. Pronounced "*Kammus*" it's probably from the Gaelic "*Cambas*", meaning bay or creek, but its actual etymology is uncertain. There was a colliery here until the mid-1960s, and aluminium was imported for smelting at nearby Lynmouth. Now it's a rather unremarkable village reflecting the uninspiring industry and wastelands surrounding it.

Eventually, I found a place where I could access the sands. I didn't expect to find anything particularly appealing here, but I was in for a surprise. I found myself on a wide beach with a spectacular horizon. The sands are about 3 miles long and bordered by high dunes and stands of pine trees so all that industry is quite concealed, and to all intents and purposes it might as well not be there at all. And it was almost deserted. I could see a lone fisherman casting into the surf, and a dog-walker or two, but that was all.

I was taken by this place. The silos at Blyth are just specks on the horizon a mile or so from here, and to the north the wide sands arc slightly past the estuary of the river Wansbeck to the low cliffs at Newbiggin beyond.

The unexpected expanse of Cambois Beach   *Photo: the author*

The Wansbeck creates little more than a wide furrow in the sand where it meets the sea. I approached a gentleman, one of the few figures on the beach and who I took to be a local only because he looked stoically indifferent to the stupendous views around him. I asked him if it is possible to wade through the estuary and he looked at me with an expression of sympathy, the sort one reserves for people not quite in possession of their faculties. Apparently, you can't.

So I took a final gaze around at the unexpected discovery of Cambois beach, and I wondered why, having been born and brought up not so many miles from here, I never knew about it before. I suppose it can only be because Blyth and its surroundings have always endured a reputation of being bleakly unappealing. That legacy now seems to me to be unfair. This is a fine, pleasant place, and in spite of the nearby industry it has the virtue of being quiet and undisturbed, an oasis of peace and space.

I went back to the car and drove back up to the main road and the bridge that crosses the Wansbeck where a pedestrian bridge also carries the England Coast Path, and then to the headland looking down onto the last part of Cambois beach, the bit I would have reached by wading the Wansbeck had I not been warned off. I ventured into the Sandy Bay Holiday Park, perched on the cliffs above the shore. It's a huge park with literally hundreds of static caravans, all painted the same pastel cream, many with little terraces tacked on and all set in a massive site with its own central bar and restaurant area. It's easy to mock these places, but to my surprise I found it extremely well-ordered, spacious, very well-kept and of course overlooking the wonderful Cambois bay. The vans themselves (it was very quiet so I could have a wander around without looking too suspicious) were clearly spacious, comfortable and no doubt equipped with all necessary conveniences. I wasn't converted, but I was impressed.

The headland before Newbiggin is known as Spital Point, and the rocky slabs and boulders that skirt its base are Spital Carrs, where great black boulders are piled up as sea defences. It's scrambling country down there.

Cambois Beach looking north over the Wansbeck estuary towards Newbiggin

Photo: the author

By the time I got to Newbiggin the Northumbrian weather was doing what it does – one thing one minute and another thing the next. After the clear blue skies of Cambois beach it had come on to rain, a nasty little drizzle that wet everything. And by the look of the sky there was more to come.

The bay is a steep crescent, enclosed by rocky man-made breakwaters. The seafront is mostly traffic-free, so I left the car in the town and walked down to the promenade, by now with the hood of my jacket up and tied firmly under my chin. Good-looking housing borders the arc of sand and the grassy slopes that lead down to it, small boats are hauled up on a hard-standing and there's a lifeboat station and one or two cafes.

Perhaps the feature for which Newbiggin is most renowned is the art installation of two figures mounted on scaffolding, 12.5 metres high, way out in the bay secured on a pile of rocks and boulders. This foundation is exposed at low tide, but when the tide is high the figures of a young man and woman appear to be standing among the waves. They are both gazing out to sea and dressed in contemporary fashion, both in blue jeans and boots, he with a flat cap and she with a rather bosomy crop top. It's created some divided opinion in the town, so I gather, but it's been there since 2007 so it looks as if it's here to stay. For those whose eyesight doesn't focus at that distance there's a smaller replica mounted on the promenade.

The Newbiggin figures "Ebb & Flo",
promenade version
Photo: Peter Adcock

Leaning on the railings gazing out at the couple on the rocks, I was by now getting very wet, and through the misty drizzle I saw that there appeared to be a café of some sort at the north end of the promenade. I headed up there, to find not only a café but the Maritime and Lifeboat Centre. I now had reason to be glad of the rain, for otherwise I might not have sought the shelter of the café and not discovered this exceptional place.

I was quite bowled over by what I found inside, unprepared for the level and quality of the exhibition. There are huge curved screen videos showing archive film of the industry of the sea, the lifeboats and daily life around the harbour. It was all accompanied by delicate, often poignant narration, poetry and music. There are dozens of exhibits, beautifully presented, and to top it all the actual lifeboat, the Mary Joicey which served 1966 – 1981.

It's huge, and you climb some stairs to get level with it so you can see inside. I spent ages there, and not because of the rain. It was so wonderful that I was moved to give them some money.

Newbiggin Bay

Photo: Claire Johnson

To the north end of the bay St Bartholomew's Church stands on Church Point. It's an attractive building sadly surrounded by a static caravan park on the headland. More reassuring is the Cresswell Arms which has a sign outside declaring itself "*the last pub before Norway*", a useful note for anyone heading that way.

The stunning exhibition at the Newbiggin Maritime & Lifeboat Centre, including the original Newbiggin Lifeboat, archive film and much more

Photos: the author

Beyond the Point the coast path wanders above a rocky shore where grey slabs with names like Snab Point, Seal Skears and Stank Letch Rocks finger out into the surf. About a mile on are the power industry's constructions at Lynmouth, the last outpost of man's modern industrial incursion on this coast that I shall encounter. Due to the restrictions imposed by the need for commercial secrecy, health and safety and the private greens of the golf course it's difficult to access the coastline here, although the Coastal Path does make a hurried pass along the clifftop. I took the car back to the road and tried to forge a way to the coast through the power station complex, but was met with security barriers, more high visibility jackets and hard hats, so I went back around it and eventually found myself above the rocky low cliffs that lead on to Cresswell a couple of miles away, and the beginning of Druridge Bay.

I wanted to see the coastline beneath the power station for the record if nothing else, and so I pulled the car over into a deserted, small car park on the cliffs and gritted my teeth in the face of the rain. I had to stumble for a hundred yards or so through high grasses and dunes which soaked my trousers, but it was worth it in the end because standing on the cliff looking back at the Lynmouth power station I could see that beneath the complex there was a wonderful bay of sand. High cliffs hide what's behind, and because it's virtually inaccessible it's deserted. Today that might have been because of the slanting rain, but I'm guessing it's probably like that even in sunnier times.

A stunning sunset over Cambois Beach captured by David Thompson

There are those who say that there is a beauty in the weather, the different light, the feel in the air. Well there isn't, and I was feeling wet and grumpy. Nevertheless, just before the village of Cresswell I pulled over again and found myself above a strange little rocky inlet. The water seemed to be brown and brackish, and in the centre of it stood a solitary heron looking doleful and bedraggled. I watched him for a while before he flapped off to find somewhere more comfortable, and standing there alone in the dunes soaked and dripping I decided to follow suit and squelched my way back to the safety of the bar at The Commissioner's Quay.

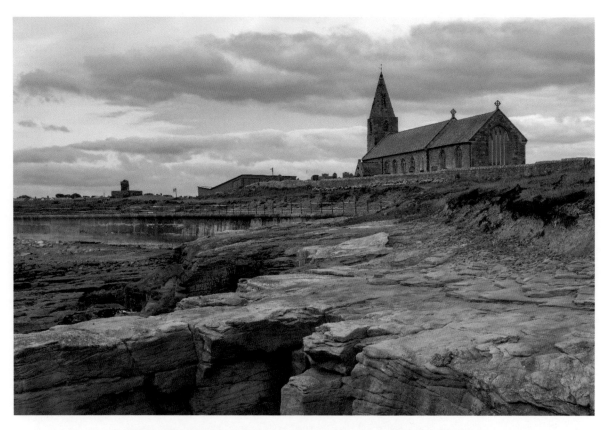

Above - St Bartholomews Church, Newbiggin point – photo: Claire Johnson
Below – sunset over Newbiggin Bay – Photo: Derek Taylor

FIVE

CRESSWELL TO ALNMOUTH

It never occurred to me that I might grow fond of the Blyth quayside with its industry and Boaty McBoatface tied up across the river, but I did, and I left this morning for my new base in Alnmouth if not with a tear in my eye certainly with a wistful memory of a place that had surprised me, in so many unexpected ways.

The weather had improved too, and by the time I got back to Cresswell where I'd left off yesterday the morning mist had lifted to sunshine and a promising day. I actually stopped off on the way to look back at the sands below Lynmouth because I wanted to confirm to myself that it is, in the sunshine as much as it appeared to be through the rain, a genuinely pleasant beach nestling in the shadow of the industrial structures. And it is.

The beach at Lynmouth – a wonderful place that belies its industrial background

Photo: Derek Taylor

Cresswell is a delightful little place, once past the approach which is lined with rows of static caravans and odd little hut-like structures I took to be holiday chalets. The beach is small but attractive in spite of the proliferation of the caravans, and the village itself is open with stone cottages beside a wide green space. There's a 15th century Pele Tower here too, a mini-castle built as a defence and refuge against persistent raiders from the borders, and more cottages line the low cliff above the coastline.

The main attraction of Cresswell for me is that it marks the beginning of what I might call "*the rural coast*". From here on there is no more industry, no more swathes of scruffy wasteland, only the countryside and coast of Northumberland, much of it just as it was a hundred years ago and more. Unless you count the small harbours at Amble, Craster, Beadnell and Seahouses, there's not a concrete promenade to disturb the dunes and sands between here and Spittal, just before Berwick. Cresswell also marks the beginning of Druridge Bay, 7 miles of sand and dunes, one of the longest continuous stretches of beach on the Northumberland coast.

Just outside Cresswell village opposite a roadside café is a small car park in the dunes. I pulled in here and stepped out into glorious sunshine and a light sea breeze. There's a hundred yards or so of sandy path through the hummocks and grasses to the sands, amidst which I discovered the somewhat ramshackle premises of the Cresswell Boat Club. It wasn't the haphazard collection of boats and rusty trailers that arrested my attention, but the Jolly Roger which was flying above the gates. If that is a measure of the members' sense of humour then I'm inclined to ask for an application form.

I emerged from the dunes onto the sands of Druridge Bay and wandered down to the water's edge. As befits a man of my age I took off my socks and shoes and rolled my trousers up. The water was warmer than I expected and I splashed along the shore feeling the soft, wet sand beneath my feet as I gazed around at the wide horizon. It's so vast, this beach, it seems that there could be no number of tourists that would make it actually crowded.

This place is such an exceptional natural resource it's hard to imagine that not so long ago in the 1980s a pressurised water nuclear reactor was planned for here, and even more recently an open cast coal mine. We have the then Communities Secretary Sajid Javid to thank for the rejection of these preposterous proposals, and now the coastline is protected by several nature reserves, the principal one being Druridge Bay Nature Reserve.

The England Coast Path and the Northumberland Coast Path wander together through the dunes, and slightly north of the centre of the sands is the Druridge Bay Country Park. There's a large car park here, a visitors' centre with a café, tourist information and within its extensive surroundings a lake formed from original open cast mining where bird life and long walks around the shore attract visitors by the literal coachload. But it's remarkable how those disgorged from the buses seem to dissipate, and I sat alone on the sands for a while with hardly a sound around me save for the gentle ploshing of the seashore and the occasional seabird's cry.

Right: The great expanse of Druridge Bay

Below: More Jolly Rogers at Low Hauxley

Photos: the author

The north end of Druridge Bay turns into Low Hauxley, and the headland before the town of Amble. I spent a little time here on the wide, flat sands. A collection of small, wooden chalets are sprinkled in the dunes above the beach, untidy but attractively eccentric. One of them had a flagpole set facing the beach flying the Jolly Roger, like the boat club back at Cresswell. Perhaps there's a strong sense of belligerent independence in the residents up here, or maybe they're just slightly bonkers, which I like to think is what it is.

I met a delightful, elderly and slightly disabled lady on the beach there. She was pottering about with her dog which was obviously getting on a bit, like his mistress. She told me that after her husband died she upped and left wherever it was she lived elsewhere in the country and decided that Low Hauxley is where she wanted to spend the rest of her days. She said she loves it here but that she missed not having as many friends. I advised her to spend more time in the pub at which she shook with laughter. I don't think she thought I was being serious.

The sands below the headland of Low Hauxley give me my first view of Coquet Island a mile off the coast with its signature lighthouse and the remains of a medieval monastery. The island is owned by the Duke of Northumberland and managed by the RSPB. It's populated by colonies of various terns and puffins and is strictly protected. Although it's possible to take boat trips out to the island the public aren't allowed to land there.

Top: *Coquet Island   Photo: David Thompson*
Above: *Approaching Amble from Low Hauxley   Photo: the author*

Flat, firm sand curves around the headland and as the coast to the north is revealed I found to my surprise that far in the distance and low on the horizon I could make out the spiky shapes of Dunstanburgh Castle. Turning round I could still see the industrial structures at Lynmouth far in the south. What a unique juxtaposition. What a panorama!

For a mile the coastline meanders above sands and rocky outcrops. Other than the general notation of Amble Links I can find no specific names for these places, unusual on this coast where almost every rock, boulder and little inlet has a name of some sort, usually of ancient derivation and often amusing. Here the coast meets the harbour at Amble, effectively the estuary of the river Coquet.

Amble is popular with holidaymakers, and visitors are well catered for with fish and chips shops, cafes and gift shops. But it's also a working harbour with a good sized quay and sheltered moorings. I had a coffee on the quay and wandered about where I saw several good-sized vessels moored amidst nets, cages, ropes and all the paraphernalia of the fishing industry. There was also a little gaggle of boats for trips around Coquet Island, and a smart marina for private yachts and the slipways and small boatyards that service them. I admit to being unimpressed by the silo-like architecture of the four apartment blocks looming over the harbour.

Amble and the river Coquet estuary at sunset

Photo: Dawn Roberts

The town is spread on the southern bank of the river which looks over to the dry-stone pier, old groynes and piles and a sandy foreshore on the other side. There is no crossing of the Coquet here and I had to travel upriver a couple of miles, following the route of the Coast Paths which are now joined by St Oswald's Way, to the bridge at Warkworth. The castle here sits high above the village with a pennant flying above the keep, although I was disappointed to see that it's not the Jolly Roger. Warkworth is a stunningly pretty village, enclosed by the horseshoe bend in the river, and from the ancient stone bridge the coastal route passes next to the golf links to rejoin the sands at Alnmouth Bay, just over the dunes I saw from the Amble side of the river.

Above: *Amble lighthouse*
Photo: Lyn Douglas

Below: *Warkworth viewed from Amble harbour*
Photo: Claire Johnson

Alnmouth Bay is another long stretch, almost as long as Druridge Bay. Wide, under high dunes, after 4 miles it meets the estuary of the river Aln which scours a wide furrow through the sand at the small town of Alnmouth. The weather had turned again, becoming threateningly unsettled, and as my windscreen wipers flicked in the drizzle I decided to head for the village and explore the bay tomorrow. My decision was about 5 minutes too late. By the time I had found a parking place close to my hotel in the notoriously difficult parking environment of Alnmouth the heavens had opened and I was trapped in my car listening to the rain drumming on the roof. The downpour was ferocious. Tourists in plastic hooded anoraks scurried for shelter or huddled under shop awnings as the deluge continued, the Northumbrian weather again reinforcing its prerogative to do whatever it damn well pleases.

Low Hauxley seascape   *Photo: Keith Hamblin*

Amble

Above *photo:*
David Thompson

Below *photo:*
the author

SIX

ALNMOUTH TO CRASTER

I've known Alnmouth for many years, since I was a child when my parents would bring me and my brother to enjoy the wide sands, and later in life I have spent many a week here with my wife for the peace and space of the coast and the countryside around. It's a place I have always held very fondly in my heart. That morning the unpleasant downpours of yesterday evening had been banished by a clear blue sky and a light breeze, so at some risk to public propriety I decided to wear my shorts.

River Aln estuary at high tide, Alnmouth   Panorama by Nathan Atkinson

You could call Alnmouth a large village or a small town, as either would be fitting. Approached from the main coast road across a four arch stone bridge its only main street wanders through old stone housing and a pleasantly eclectic mix of cafés, gift shops and pubs until reaching the end overlooking the estuary of the river Aln. There's a place to sit here, a small garden with a couple of bench seats and an information board, looking out over the coastline. It's called *"Dr Joy's Garden",* a memorial to the late Dr Joy Edelman, respected cardiologist and resident of the town. The garden is a favourite place of mine and I walked down there to relax for a while and enjoy the space. From the seats here the whole coastline was spread before me. From the mound of Church Hill on the other side of the estuary with its cross marking the site of an ancient church, far to the south across the wide bay the low, grey shapes of the harbour wall and rooftops of Amble were just visible. Inland the pennant at Warkworth Castle flew high above distant woodland, and out to sea, low on the horizon, I could see Coquet Island with its lighthouse, seals and seabirds.

The passage of time, tide and storm has vastly changed the geography of the estuary over the years. There used to be a functioning port here where grain, wool and other goods were shipped. There's little evidence of that now, just the sands and mud flats at low tide.

There's a walk from here which loops around the back of the village alongside the estuary and past the yacht station, little more than a few dinghies pulled up onto the shore, sails furled and the rigging tinkling in the breeze. The path is called "*Lovers' Walk*", but being on my own that day I had to use my imagination. That wasn't hard to do while the sun glistened on the water. It's a wide panorama with views across to the rising western countryside of Northumberland. Eider ducks, oystercatchers, dippers with their incessant foraging, even swans congregate here, and frequently a solitary heron standing dead still, watching the water.

Then a short stroll brought me to the four-arched bridge, back down the high street and onto the sands.

Lovers' Walk approaches the 4-arch bridge at Alnmouth Photo: the author

My Ordnance Survey map shows that although the route of the Coast Path takes the rambler around the estuary and over the four arch bridge, there is a dotted line marking a way through the estuary channel in the sands. I've seen this river mouth many times, both at high tide when it's a torrent, and at low water when it seems to be little more than a trickle, and I've often wondered if it is possible to wade across as the O.S. map suggests you can, or whether it's a mischief of the Ordnance Survey people at the expense of the walking community. As I walked down to the sands through the grasses and dunes the tide was as far out as I've ever seen it, and when I spotted a gentleman of indeterminate age impeccably dressed in cream bags, a paisley cravat and a straw hat, I naturally engaged him in conversation. He alleged himself a local, but spoke with a soft, Scottish accent and appeared as if he ought to be in a bar with a martini rather than wandering a beach in Northumberland so I have no idea if that was true. Anyway, when I asked him about fording the estuary he was quite specific. On no account should such a thing be attempted due to the depth, the current and all sorts of otherwise hidden perils. As he earnestly imposed this caution on me, behind him I could see a Dad, a young boy of about 6 and a small dog happily splashing through the channel. They easily made it to the other side.

Below *–Alnmouth estuary sunset*   *Photo: Lyn Douglas*

The beach continues north from Alnmouth, past the car park behind the dunes and beneath the golf courses of Alnmouth village and Foxton, passing old wooden groynes and breakwaters in the sands. After a mile or so I arrived at the rocky promontory of Seaton Point. I avoided clambering about on the rocks by taking a path around and above it through of a cluster of static caravans before returning to the shore and continuing on to the hamlet of Boulmer. The coastline here is mainly rocky and shingle, with occasional patches of sand marked by outcrops with typically intriguing names – Marmouth Scars, North Reins and Red Ends. Offshore a gap in these rocky formations creates an entrance to a small, natural harbour below the village where there is a short stretch of sand and seaweed with small boats and rusty trailers pulled up amidst boxes, crates, nets and an old tractor that probably offers a challenge to anyone who might want to try to start it.

Boulmer (pronounced "*Boomer*" if you wish to integrate) consists of a row of only a dozen or so stone houses lining the low cliff and a few cottages on the approach road, but it does have The Fishing Boat Inn, and a reputation for having been the smuggling capital of this coastline.

In the 18th and early 19th centuries the government imposed taxes on a range of goods from lace and tea to spirits and tobacco which were so high that smuggling was a highly profitable occupation. But a conviction for smuggling frequently attracted the death penalty, and so remote, quiet coastlines were prized by those who engaged in such activities. Gangs came from across the border, "*Boomer Men*" they were called, typically from the gypsy community and famously from Kirk Yetholm just over the border some 50 miles to the west. Kirk Yetholm, now renowned for being the northern end of the Pennine Way, was then a headquarters for a prodigious smuggling community. There are long and prolific stories about all this, and the complicity and collaborations that went with a divided local community, but it has a particular fascination for me as nearly 200 years ago, between 1826 and 1846, my 3x great grandfather was a commissioned coastguard stationed at Low Newton, just a few miles up the coast, charged with disrupting the activities of such men and bringing them to justice. I've often wondered if he ever came face to face with the Boomer Men. I expect he did.

Boulmer   *Photo: Lyn Douglas*

The Fishing Boat Inn is in the middle of the row of houses lining the low cliff, set back from the road with a small stone walled car park in front. Beyond, slabs of rocky fingers stretch out into the sea. The crescent of sand is piled with heaps of brown seaweed among the boats, tackle and the tractor. At the back of the pub is a wooden terrace veranda where I took a coffee and sat watching the sea glisten in calm sunshine. A pair of cormorants sat on rocks exposed offshore. There was not another soul to be seen. The air was full of silence.

A grassy path leads from Boulmer above the low cliffs and rocky slabs of Boulmer Steel. It skirts meadow-like farmland and before long arrives at the unspoiled, breathtaking beauty of Sugar Sands and Howdiemont Sands. These two little adjacent crescent bays are not easily discovered, and those in the know will probably deny their existence. They are accessed only by the coast path, or by a discreetly signposted track from the nearby village of Longhoughton. Because of my schedule I'd brought the car, negotiated the narrow track and the actual farm through which it passes, and left it with only two or three others on the grass behind the dunes. I settled myself with my back on a grassy hummock and my bare feet in the warm sand. The surf ploshed on the shore, seabirds cried occasionally, and I sat in undisturbed peace.

I had almost snoozed off in the sun when my attention was alerted to a young couple trying to launch a 2-man inflatable kayak of some sort. It looked like their first time with it as there seemed to be a lot of activity with little progress before they tentatively pushed it into the water and shoved off. There was then a good deal of uncoordinated paddling as they cautiously wobbled out in to the bay.

The remote beauty of Sugar Sands

Photo: the author

As the kayakers were crabbing about offshore an elderly looking gentleman reversed a tractor and a trailer down the beach with a sizeable launch and big twin outboards on the back. I could see he was dressed in a colourful Malibu shirt, sandals and a straw hat. This looked so encouraging that I went and got my binoculars from the car. After slipping the boat off the trailer into the shallows, he drove the tractor back up the sand, returned to the boat, and then drove slowly away from the shallows. Some 50 yards or so offshore he pushed the throttle open, the bow lifted and the boat powered out, turned right and with a great wake from the mighty engines he headed south down the coast and disappeared beyond the Boulmer headland. I would have given much to know who he was, where he was headed, what was his business of the day.

In the meantime, there was much unbalanced floundering from the kayak, and I am embarrassed to admit that I was mildly disappointed they didn't fall out.

A short distance from the crescent bays, perched right on the edge of the cliff, is the little cottage known as the Bathing House. Formerly used as accommodation and a bathing facility for nearby Howick Hall, it's now renovated, modernised and used as a holiday let. Below is the extraordinary topography of Howick Haven and Rumbling Kern, where nature has carved and eroded this place into a series of little coves, remarkable rock formations, tiny sandy bays and secret hiding places. I lingered here a while watching the sea gurgling around the rock-holes, took some photographs, and watched a small party of schoolchildren in high visibility jackets and hard hats being given what I imagine was a better geography lesson than they would have received by sitting in a classroom with a text book.

Above – *the bathing house at Howick frames the spiky ruins of Dunstanburgh Castle*
Photo: Ant Clark

Left – *Rumbling Kern at Howick Haven*
Photo: Derek Taylor

The path continues along the clifftop above rocky slabs and steels to Cullernose Point where the O.S. map provides more intriguing names for the coastal features of Black Hole and Hole o' the Dyke, and eventually arrives at Craster, famous for a quaint, compact harbour, for kippers, crabs and the Jolly Fisherman.

The harbour at Craster   *Photo: the author*

Images of Alnmouth

Above the estuary

Below the town
across the estuary
from Church Hill

Photos: Lyn Douglas

SEVEN

CRASTER TO LOW NEWTON

During an overnight break back at The Schooner Hotel in Alnmouth, I met two more of our photographers. Both The Schooner and The Red Lion just up the road have delightful terraces, decking overlooking the estuary where one can sit and enjoy the views. It was an evening of still air and setting sun. As we were talking about the wonderful colours of the sky I was reminded that capturing a sunrise over the estuary at this time of year involves being up and about at 4.00.a.m, at which my admiration for their dedication increased dramatically, but I'm not personally afflicted with that level of insanity.

Craster: two stubby, stone piers enclose a small harbour, a narrow crescent of sand and shingle at high water when small boats swing lazily on the their mooring ropes. At low tide it's oozy, exposed ropes and chains snake over the mud and seaweed, and mooring buoys lie sideways waiting for the flood. Boats are pulled up above the high water mark below a small lifeboat station and grassy banks on the north side provide places to sit, watch, and absorb the sea air.

It's a small fishing harbour and in the quietness of the off-season months during autumn and winter the business of the day passes at a calm, effortless pace. In high season it's popular with tourists, the little streets are often crowded, and for those arriving by car with collapsible chairs and inflatable canoes parking can be impossible within the village. Vehicles are relegated to a dedicated out-of-

Craster Harbour
Photo: Claire Johnson

town car park, and when that's full a local farmer just up the country approach road augments his subsidies by opening the gate into his fields.

Apart from the quaint beauty of the harbour and the coastline, three things commend Craster in particular. Kippers, of course, which are the dominion of the Robson family here since 1890. The fish is sourced from Norway these days, so I'm told, but it's smoked in the oily premises overlooking the harbour and a shop offers visitors the opportunity to enjoy the kipper experience, one that often lingers a bit longer than expected. The Jolly Fisherman is just over the road, overlooking the coastline and the rocks of Muckle Carr which underpin the low cliff. It's a pub with great appeal to me, timbered and open fired with high stools at a bar lined with pumps and glasses where I can rest an elbow.

Perhaps most iconic is the view from Craster to the spiky ruins of Dunstanburgh Castle, a mile to the north. The road around the harbour passes in front of a row of white cottages, most with the rosettes and window stickers of the tourist rental, and then ends at a gate which leads onto the grassy path to the castle. Right then, in July 2021, as coronavirus restrictions were easing but travel abroad was largely curtailed, many were forsaking the delights of Benidorm and Teneriffe for places such as this and the line of shorts and sunhats snaked along the clifftop path like a cinema queue.

A stunning view of Dunstanburgh Castle by Ant Clark

But it's not always like this. The castle is quite inaccessible by vehicle, save perhaps for the 4x4s of English Heritage who are currently charged with its upkeep. The walk along the grassy, sheepy, clifftop path brings Dunstanburgh ever closer, looming larger with every step until standing beneath the massive gatehouse one can imagine its powerful influence in days gone by.

The great gatehouse of Dunstanburgh Castle, even in ruins, is resonant of the power it once held
*Photos **above**: Ant Clark   **below**: Darren Chapman*

The castle has a deep and complex history, and for those so inclined there's much to read and discover about it. Suffice it to say here that construction was begun in the 14th century by Thomas, Earl of Lancaster as a protestation against King Edward II. Built on a headland formed by an outcrop of the Great Whin Sill it offered a promising defensive location, although not, as it turned out, an impregnable one.

Lancaster was defeated before he was able to make much use of his seat, and the castle passed to John O'Gaunt who strengthened it as a protection against raiders from the north, the unruly and irritatingly persistent Scots. During the Wars of the Roses between the Yorkists and the Lancastrians in the 15th century its allegiance changed hands several times and it was assaulted, battered, sieged, and had cannon fired at it until it fell to bits. It never recovered, and has lain in ruins ever since.

It's a huge site, not apparent from the approach. In its heyday the great walls enclosed an interior which held a market, housing, barracks, supplies and all the offices of living and for the administration of the lands around. Now only some exterior walls, the great gatehouse and a tower known as Lilburn tower remain. Nevertheless, the castle still holds a majesty, resonant of knights in armour, heraldic pennants, heroic deeds and bravery. It seems to hold a defiance, down but not out, and its dramatic, distinctive ruins silhouetted against the skyline can be seen for miles up and down the coast. Today it's a place to wander about and imagine the past, the transience of power and war set against a backdrop of unassailable, unconquerable nature.

Above - *History and modernity – golfers play under the castle at Dunstanburgh / Photo: Claire Johnson* *Below* *– the castle from Embleton Bay / Photo: the author*

In days gone by there was a small harbour and moorings here, for supply or escape as the case may be. They are long gone now and around the feet of the great gatehouse, walls that still stand heavy and resilient, the path leads over rocks and boulders down to the sands of Embleton Bay.

Taking its name from the village nearly a mile inland at the centre of the curve of sand, Embleton Bay runs for a mile and a half to the low rocks before Low Newton, and the small crescent sands of the haven there, known as Newton Haven or St Mary's Haven. Embleton is a fine beach, typically Northumbrian with soft, dry, floury sand below the dunes

running into a line of brown and yellow wrack at high-water mark, then flat and damp where foot and paw prints are left to fade slowly into the wet sand near the shore. I wandered down and left my own memories, and there was hardly a soul in sight in spite of the lines along the cliff from Craster.

There are tracks through the dunes half-way along the beach, up to the manicured green of the golf course, only as wide as the first tee here where diamond-pullovered golfers wait for leisurely walkers to saunter by on their right of way. The low clubhouse is set into the dunes here with some limited parking for those unwilling or unable to make the walk from Craster or from Low Newton in the north. From here the long, narrow lane leads up to the village. Historic development has followed the lines of the roads and lanes, rather than any planned pattern, and so Embleton is pleasingly irregular, and with no fewer than three pubs, The Greys with its attractive, flowery garden, The Blue Bell which I reluctantly confess to having never been in, and The Dunstanburgh Castle Hotel.

The splendour of Embleton Bay caught by David Thompson

The outlet of the Embleton Burn scours a shallow channel through the sands just past the golf course, but unlike the Wansbeck it's easily fordable on foot, and a leisurely amble takes me to the bay at Low Newton, its freshwater ponds and small nature reserve behind the dunes.

Low Newton is probably the most original of all the villages on the coast. There is no new development here, only the original three-sided enclave of the little hamlet and a few cottages spread up the hill approach. It's intensely pretty with a square of green in the centre lined with white stones, opening directly onto the wide sands of Newton Haven. Approached from the coast road through High Newton and then down a hill to the village, it's one way in and one way out, and no visitor traffic at all is allowed. Set in the corner of the whitewashed enclave is The Ship, a small, white-painted original inn that has been here for more than 200 years. Now it's popular with visitors, brews its own distinctive ales, and has even been visited by HRH Prince Charles. He apparently took a beer here, and there's a somewhat unofficial "By Appointment" plaque in the bar that looks as if was probably knocked up by the landlord after a celebratory session.

The village has a long history of smuggling and the coastguards who policed it. Nearly 200 years ago in 1826, my 3 x great grandfather was posted here as a commissioned coastguard, and for a time lived in the squat little cottage on the hill that overlooks the village and the coast, known then as The Watch House, but today as Lookout Cottage. He stayed here with his wife for 20 years, raised 7 children, and survived the weather, the smugglers, the dangers of the North Sea and no doubt the pease pudding and stottie cake. I stayed in that cottage myself 2 years ago when researching my earlier book, and the views from up there over Embleton Bay to the spiky fingers of Dunstanburgh Castle on the distant headland are simply spectacular.

The quaint, green square of Low Newton – Photo: the author

It's sobering to imagine this place 200 years ago. The green square of grass in the village where the pub erects colourful parasols in summer was once the midden, the pit into which the villagers discarded their waste, the fish heads, rotting carcasses and the effluence of the privies. The cottages themselves were hovels, filthy, without facilities of any sort, crammed with fishing gear and the stench of fish, lodging seasonal workers and even pigs. In 1873 the Alnwick Rural Sanitary Authority condemned the place, describing it as *"deficient in any sanitary contrivance"*. As I wandered about amidst the carbon fibre walking poles and reflective sunglasses I could imagine unsmiling figures in shabby shawls and heavy, black boots, a squalid place and literally 200 years from ourselves.

I spent a little time at Low Newton, busy as it was with tourists enjoying the sands, the pub and the appealing ambience of the sea-shore. But there's busy and busy. There are no Blackpool crowds here. There is space for a dog to chase a ball, for a child to build his sandcastles, and for a peaceful delay on the sand watching the vast horizon of sea and sky.

I walked up the grassy hill to Lookout Cottage and stood beside it gazing at the view down the coast, exactly the same as it was 2 years ago, and indeed as it would have been 200 years ago as my 3x great grandfather scanned the horizon for the masts of Dutch trading ships which might pause a while to allow the discharge of a few barrels of this and that into the waiting boats of the Boomer Men.

Views up to Lookout Cottage, and down from it over Newton Haven and Embleton Bay to Dunstanburgh Castle   Photos: the author

EIGHT

LOW NEWTON TO SEAHOUSES

The site of Lookout Cottage was well chosen by those responsible in the coastguard service back in the early 19th century. High on Newton Point it has clear views of the coast and out to sea, and north over Beadnell Bay, where my journey will now take me.

It's a familiar, Northumbrian, arc of sand. It's as if such bays go on and on, one after another - the dunes, the arc of sand, the firmer, flatter, darker brown towards the shoreline, the headland in the distance beyond which will be another bay, another long crescent, another headland.

But do not be deceived, each is different. Each bay has its own detail, its own personality. How else is it possible to have a favourite? I declared this Beadnell Bay to be one of mine. I might even have said my *very* favourite. That is, save for one, but I did not know that then as I had not yet arrived there.

Below The Point, enclosed by the outcrops of Pern Carr and Snook Point is Football Hole, a small bay of rocks and sand so called because, I'm told, the game was played nearby in some days past. Northumberland is the master, or perhaps the mistress, of hidden gems like this, hardly known, discreet places where one can find solitude on a patch of sand with only the sound of the sea and seabirds to keep you company. But Football Hole is but a prelude to the bay that follows, Beadnell, and it is surely a sight to lift any heart and clear a head of any lingering excesses.

In the morning, having returned to Low Newton with a re-packed car, for my base moved onward that day, the coast was presented in a way I cannot recall ever having seen before. It was flat, mirror calm, not a ripple on its surface as far as the eye could see. There was not a breath of wind. Others I passed by today commented on it too. A morning haze slightly obscured the horizon so that the line of the sea, or at least where one would expect that line to be, blended into the skyline, and a fishing boat far out appeared to be floating in the air, ethereal, ghostly. I went down to the sands just where the bay begins after Snook Point. The water lapped at the shoreline in a lazy flollop and for the second time on this journey I removed my shoes and paddled contentedly along the shore. The crowds of yesterday were a distant memory, the bay almost deserted save for waders and dippers at the shoreline, busy and unconcerned with my presence.

Half way along the beach is Long Nanny, not a disreputable relative but a water course that channels its little estuary in the sands. It can be forded, but I would have had to take off more than my shoes, and in spite of the lack of onlookers you never know who might appear from the dunes, so I decided to avoid any misunderstandings and sought the footbridge just a hundred yards inland.

Left: *Beadnell harbour*
Photo: Anne Nicholson

The beach continues under dunes, sections of them high enough to form sandy cliffs, and the little harbour at Beadnell draws closer. I could see a cluster of dinghies and people on the beach there. Beadnell is a small seaside town, unmistakably touristy with many static caravans and even some new housing development, an unusual feature on this coast. But the coastline itself is not much troubled by that, and the small harbour with its old brick 19th century lime kilns, small quayside and boats is an appealing place.

I strolled around the harbour where the kilns are fascinating features of an industry long abandoned, their cave-like entrances now piled with nets and fishermen's pots. For a while I leaned on the harbour wall for the view back down the bay. I could see the fingers of Dunstanburgh's ruins in the distance, and even Lookout Cottage on the hill above Low Newton. In the dead calm a small fishing boat left its wake in the sea like dark slashes in a velvet coat.

Behind the harbour is a tourists' car park, an information centre, toilets and places for coffee and food. There's also a windsurf shop, but in the calm of the day I expected they would be in the pub.

There's a path from the harbour that squeezes round the back of the kilns and old stone walls, then between the clifftop and some housing to a green headland, a long spit of grass which tapers out from the shore, becoming a rocky, narrow finger before its raking slabs dip beneath the water. This is St Ebb's Nook, the unlikely site of a small 13th century church, and there is evidence of one much earlier, from the 7th century. Remnants of the black and yellow floor and foundation stones can be found among the grasses, and a thoughtful heritage board offers information about who St Ebb was and the history of this place.

Stunning views of Beadnell Bay

Right: *photo by David Thompson*

Left: *photo by Keith Hamblin*

Above: Beadnell harbour **Below** *a dead calm sea from Ebb's Nook across Lady's Hole towards Seahouses*
Photos: the author

The view from The Nook, which allows one to walk quite a way out from the coastline itself, is extensive and for the first time the Farne Islands appeared, low on the horizon off Seahouses to the north. It was very quiet here and with the sea dead calm there was no sound of surf or breakers. I stood alone on this ancient site of religious dedication amidst a silent landscape, imagining the history that this place witnessed so many centuries ago.

My map identifies the coastal features here, *"Faggot"*, *"Nacker Hole"* and the surprising *"Lady's Hole"*, names which seem to have an ancient, vernacular derivation. Or perhaps, I wonder, the O.S. cartographers were having a particularly mischievous afternoon. In spite of extensive inquiry I have not been able to discover what *"Nacker"* means, or who the Lady was.

The sands between Beadnell and Seahouses are known as Annstead Links and curve pleasantly for a mile and a half beneath the dunes towards North Sunderland Point where the headland forms cliffs below the green of the golf course and water-filled old quarrying holes. It's quite a complicated coastline here, so I took the car into Seahouses and my new base at The Bamburgh Castle Inn which turned out to be a fine building overlooking the harbour, and I set off from there to explore.

I wandered around the harbour, lined with low storage buildings and old cottages now renovated and many let out to visitors. Those who take these places for their holidays have wonderful views out across the harbour to the Farne Islands. I took the path around the headland and over the golf links to the clifftop where I could look back down the bay to Beadnell. Below the grass of the links on the clifftop path there was a commotion of activity from colonies of seabirds clinging to the sandy cliff face, many with young, incessantly coming and going, the air swarming with birds and a cacophony of shrieking. The tide was out and exposed the wide, rocky slabs, boulders and shingle which fringe the base of the cliff. Then I walked back and out along the south pier, a concrete breakwater which, together with the north pier creates a wide, well-guarded haven. Small yachts and dinghies lay on the wet sand and mud flats. Later they will be lifted by the incoming water and swing gently on their mooring lines.

Seahouses harbour- photo: Keith Hamblin

A secondary arm of the north pier forms a small, deeper anchorage and embarking points. Among a few working fishing vessels there are several boats which ferry visitors out to the Farne Islands, and on the quayside I counted no less than 7 wooden kiosks offering excursions to the islands. There was a bustle of people around the harbour, and trade for the boat trips and the few coffee and ice-cream outlets seemed brisk.

I was not much interested in walking into the town itself, knowing from the drive in that it was crowded. But The Olde Ship Inn is right next door to my hotel and it's a pub that seems to be very highly regarded by the many I've heard mention it, especially those who seem to make the assessment of pubs a speciality of theirs, so it seemed sensible to take this opportunity to see what it was all about.

The Ship has a small bar, wooden and cosy and unbelievably fussy. There are things hanging, mounted, and displayed anywhere and everywhere. I could spend an afternoon, and nearly did, just gazing around at it all. There are intricate models of trawlers suspended from the ceiling and on display shelves, detailed to the most extraordinary degree. There are anchors, ships' brasses of every description, model galleons and even a brass diving helmet next to the bar. I've never seen a place so crowded with artefacts, copper and brass, delicate rigging and boats perfectly modelled down to the rivets. Down a corridor to the cosy back room there's more, and to crown it all the Hadrian Border Brewery's Farne Island beer was on fine form.

The terrace at the Bamburgh Castle Inn. The Olde Ship is the brown building just poking out from the left hand side of the hotel – conveniently close. Photo: the author

After dinner as the evening light was drawing to a close I went to sit on the hotel terrace overlooking the harbour. The dusk was still and slightly misty, the sea as calm as it been during the day and a luminescent turquoise on the horizon marked the dwindling moments of daylight. The lights of the harbour came on and small boats with their pinpricks of light drifted out across the water. The Farne Islands were smudges on the horizon out to sea, and north on the coast Bamburgh Castle loomed in the gathering twilight, a shadow on the skyline. I sat for a long while, an evening digestif close at hand, allowing my thoughts to wander, and as the light faded and the quiet harbour twinkled and shimmered I spent the most pleasant couple of hours I've had for a long time.

The Bamburgh Castle Inn overlooking the harbour at Seahouses. The building in front with the arches, on top of which is the hotel terrace, used to house lime kilns
Photo: The Inn Collection Group

NINE

THE FARNE ISLANDS

Today did not turn out as scheduled, as I had intended to wander up to Bamburgh and on to Budle Bay. However, I'd been writing a blog about this journey on my Facebook page and one of my followers posted, a bit sternly I thought, that to write about the Northumberland coast and miss out the Farne Islands would be nothing less than a travesty. When I arose this morning I realised she was right, so before breakfast I ambled down to the kiosks on the quayside here at Seahouses where they offer this sort of adventure. The day was almost cloudless but a bit of a breeze disturbed the calm of yesterday and the sea looked a bit ruffled, so as I'm not a particularly good sailor I selected the kiosk that seemed to be operating the biggest boat, a boat with a toilet, and a skipper who hadn't over-indulged the night before. I booked myself a trip and went back to the hotel terrace to sit and pass some time before my ship weighed anchor. (The picture of the seagull I've included here is incidental, but he was very persistent and I'm sure he was after my breakfast. I've called him Jonathan, obviously).

I hadn't visited Seahouses before, save for passing by on the way elsewhere, and I've always thought of it as being rather touristy with too many shops selling souvenir tat and acres of amusements and fish and chips. But it isn't like that at all and I was really starting to get drawn to it. This terrace, the view over the harbour to the Farnes, and of course The Olde Ship Inn were all conspiring to make me feel very warm towards it. I like its charm, I like its mix of fishing, tourist boats and sailing dinghies. In that context, and rather like Amble, its unashamed pursuit of the tourist dollar is not particularly troubling.

Actually, I was a bit apprehensive about the trip. I imagined sitting shoulder to shoulder on a boat crammed full of tourists, pitching and rolling, which was not an appealing prospect. I thought I might be sick, or the child squeezed in next to me might be, which would probably be worse.

Jonathan Seagull
Photo: the author

Anyway, when the time came I wandered back down to the kiosks and joined a group of people shepherded up the quay by the lady in charge, and at the end we made our way down stone steps to the boat, which was plastic and called Serenity. I stepped off the quay onto the boat following a very reluctant dog, whining and pulling on its leash, which did little to allay my fears. If the dog was sick, odds on it would be on my foot.

Once on board my fears were quite alleviated. Serenity was a broad beamed, double hull affair with masses of room to move around and observe the passing seascape. The skipper, who also provided an informative commentary – all credit to him for making it fresh and interesting given that he did it several times a day, day in and day out - turned out to be a young, bushy-bearded Australian and his mate a Scottish teacher who did this in the holidays. It did occur to me that we weren't actually in the school holidays, but I thought it best not to say anything about that.

I sat at the front of the square shaped bow under the wheelhouse and, as it turned out, one of the loudspeakers used for the commentary, so I was constantly well-informed. It takes about 20 minutes to reach the first of the islands, Inner Farne, and as we motored closer and then further out and around the islands we had wonderful views all around us. The breeze out on the sea was not as chilly as I had thought it might be, and Serenity seemed to cope well with what little swell there was. The dog lay quietly under a seat and, so far as I was aware, was not sick on anyone.

The Farne Islands, from Seahouses harbour
Photo: James Lamb

The skipper skilfully manoeuvred the boat to within only a yard or two of the islands, some large, some little more than outcrops of rock protruding only a foot or so out of the water. There are about 20 islands in the Farnes group, depending on the state of the tide. We observed colonies of grey seals lying on the rocks and occasionally flopping off into the water, right next to us. The crystal-clear sea gurgled around the boat as we wallowed gently by the rocks. We saw dolphins playing not far from the boat, and I wondered if they might even be the same ones as those I saw off the headland at Tynemouth, not that unlikely so I'm told, but as I didn't know them by name I couldn't ask. It was a genuinely wonderful experience.

We went to Longstone, the furthest out of the Farnes, famous for the heroism of Grace Darling in the wreck of the S.S. Forfarshire way back in 1838. It was quite poignant to float around offshore just under the lighthouse and imagine those events so long ago, and to think that my ancestors from Bamburgh at that time might have had a hand in the return of the small number of

Dolphins captured by Amanda Fall

survivors to shore, and that my 3 x great grandfather, the coastguard down the coast at Low Newton, may have done so too. Longstone is a large installation now with steel buildings clustered around the base of the lighthouse tower. We were told by the Australian skipper that

Some islands peek just above the waves, where seals bask in the sun – photo: the author

it is all solar powered now, fully automated, and therefore unoccupied save for occasional maintenance. It's such a natural, peaceful place that if Trinity House offered me a job living there pottering about and looking after things, I'd probably do it for nothing. At least in this weather I would, but I expect that Grace Darling might have had a thing or two to say about the conditions here in full storm, crashing waves and howling wind.

Although landing on the islands had not been permitted during the Coronavirus restrictions, it had been re-instated not long before my visit, and it was again possible to land on Inner Farne and explore the Puffin holes and around the old buildings on the island. However, the adventure I had booked did not include landing and so we sailed around, finding ourselves constantly surrounded by flocks of flying birds, mainly puffins with their distinctive beaks and furious wings. As we approached Staple Island, selected by the skipper because it's heavily colonised by puffins, it took me a little while to realise that the eye-watering stench that wafted over the sea was not coming from the chap sitting next to me, but from the Puffins. Their droppings are acrid, pungent like a strong fertilizer, and it pervades the air for hundreds of yards off the island. It's foul, and I'm not coming back as a puffin, or anything that has to live within half a mile of one.

Photo: Lyn Douglas

Puffin photo: James Lamb

I noticed with some surprise that some of the islands, especially Inner Farne, are green with grasses and low vegetation. The skipper's mate told me that the islands have to be managed to prevent the bird's habitat from becoming overgrown. Over the last 18 months or so the Coronavirus problem prevented proper maintenance (although I'm at a bit of a loss to understand why) and unchecked vegetation was imposing on the birds' nesting habitat. Now a program was in place to cut back all the new growth and give the birds space. It's quite a paradox, is it not, that a place we regard as purely natural and go to great lengths to protect from human interference, cannot exist as it is without the hand of man?

Knowing that the islands are strictly protected I was surprised to see a couple of private yachts anchored in an inlet of Inner Farne. But apparently it's permissible, and I imagine that if one has the means there would be much pleasure to be had in a stiff one on the poop deck as the sun goes down over the islands, gently rolling on the swell with not another soul for miles except the seals and seabirds.

Longstone

Photo:
James Lamb

Anyway, I did not get cold, or wet. I was not sick, I did not need the toilet, and I did not drop my phone overboard (which was a genuine and constant concern). I had a genuinely enthralling and quite unforgettable experience. I did comment to the skipper's mate that this was all very well in the relative calm of today, but what, I asked him, about rough weather when the boat would surely roll and buck about, rain and spray would lash the deck and the little on board facility might be in more demand than it is today. I asked him how bad it had to get before the tours were cancelled, and he simply shrugged and said they are out in all weathers, that little deters them. I don't think that would be for me at all, and I'm not sure whether the average, usually land-lubbing, tourist who endures this trip in a howling gale is to be admired or certified.

Inner Farne   *Photo: James Lamb*

The Farne Islands are a tremendous feature of the Northumberland coastline, an important heritage and natural resource, and I'm indeed grateful for the advice which avoided me missing it, which would have been unforgiveable.

Back on the hotel terrace I met another of our collaborating photographers, James Lamb. James has a particular interest in the Farnes and the birdlife, especially the Puffins. His photography is astonishing and I'm delighted to be able to showcase some of it here. Then I squeezed one in at The Olde Ship before dinner, and afterwards sat again on the terrace and the light was once more luminescent, the air calm, and Seahouses again became my unexpected heaven.

TEN

SEAHOUSES TO LINDISFARNE

I accidentally awoke at 5.30.a.m. this morning and thought I might take advantage of this unusual event by catching the sunrise over the Farne Islands, but looking out of the hotel window all I could see was fog, so dense I couldn't see the harbour 50 yards away. By 8.30 it had lifted to a heavy sea fret, and it improved as the day went on, but there was always a misty haze in the air today. After breakfast I sat on the hotel terrace overlooking the harbour and watched the boats taking visitors out to the Farne Islands, hazy shapes low on the horizon. It was again mirror calm and the boats left sharp, dark gashes behind them.

I was sitting there checking my emails and reviewing my blog when I received yet another stern reprimand, not from one of my followers this time but from several of them. Yesterday I recklessly remarked that the Scottish teacher who was working as the skipper's mate on the Farne Islands boat during the school holidays might have been doing a bit of moonlighting, the schools not actually being on holiday yet. I was informed by a number of people that, in Scotland, the schools had already broken up for the holidays, and that the gentleman's activities were perfectly legitimate. I am unfit to write this stuff really.

Looking north from the terrace I could see the edge of the town before it gives way to the road up to Bamburgh. A few hundred yards away the gable end of the St Aiden's Hotel, some unappealing apartment architecture and coastal housing peters out above the beginning of the wide arc of the bay. Rocky slabs and boulders sweep far out at low tide where rock pools gather weed and crabs. Children sometimes mooch over the rocks lifting stones, hoping to startle some hapless creature, but mostly it's the domain of quietly busy seabirds, foraging in the pools and patches of sand. The high dunes bordering the beach lose substance in the mist and Bamburgh Castle itself appears only dimly in the distance.

I said goodbye to Jonathan who had been eyeing me from the terrace wall as usual, and checked out of the hotel, ready to move on north to a new base at The Lindisfarne Inn on the road to Holy Island. Then I took myself down to the sands where the housing of Seahouses ends and the bay begins.

I kept to the beach and walked on St Aiden's sands and amongst the towering dunes by snaking, sandy paths, and on up northwards. It's a walk of considerable beauty, the wide, empty beach and the Farne Islands lying low offshore. Surprisingly, the castle is out of sight for much of the walk up from Seahouses, such is the height of the dunes above the beach, but eventually it looms into view. It's probably still at least half a mile away, but it asserts its presence even from here presiding over the coastline with a curious mix of threat and protection, as was intended when it was built centuries ago. It's probably the most photographed and written about castle in Northumberland, if not on the whole of the English coastline, so there's not much point in me trying to add my tuppence-worth to that, but it's there, and it is a sight to behold.

Left: Bamburgh Castle looms out of the mist, from the beach to the north
Photo: the author

Below: the castle presides over the village of Bamburgh
Photo: Keith Hamblin

There are so many wonderful photos of Bamburgh Castle, but it's hard to resist including this glorious image from Anne Nicholson…….

……or the beautiful atmosphere of the beach at Bamburgh with the Farne Islands just visible offshore, captured by Claire Marshall

Even in the misty fret of the morning there were many on the beach beneath and around the castle, mainly because it's so easily accessible from the village itself, a supremely pretty place with a wide green beneath the castle where cricket is played, quaint cottages and a couple of notable pubs, not least The Lord Crewe named for the man who, many years ago, took on the dilapidated castle and tried to make a community resource of it as a hospice, a school and suchlike. The castle had long been assaulted by the Scots with tedious persistence, and in the Wars of the Roses the Yorkists had fired cannon at it until it fell to bits, like Dunstanburgh. By the time Lord Crewe, the Bishop of Durham, arrived with his altruism it was almost beyond restoration, and it was not until 1894 that it was acquired by the industrialist, inventor and arms dealer William George Armstrong, later Baron Armstrong of Cragside, who shovelled money into it and made it his family seat, which it remains to this day. The castle and the village do attract coachloads of visitors, but the sands below it are long and wide especially at low tide, and it's easy to walk just a short way up the sands away from the balls and windbreaks, to feel some solace and peace. I sat for a while on a tussock of dune with my feet in the sand and just gazed around. The mist had lifted slightly and I could make out the Farnes out to sea, Inner Farne with its low, white lighthouse and the ruined chapel, out to Longstone in the distance. To the north I could make out the castle on Holy Island and far beyond through the haze the distinctive coastline of Berwick and its pinnacle chimney at Spittal, not far from my final destination, the border with Scotland. But there's much more to come between here and there.

Bamburgh Castle from the air – Photo: Will Marshall

I collected the car and drove back through Bamburgh, around the cricket green and under the great walls which seem to grow out of the rock itself, then down a little road called The Wyndings which leads out of the village to the north end of the sands. I left the car there and set off on foot. The castle could be seen dimly out of the mist to the south – more atmospheric in this natural setting than George Lucas could ever design a film set. At the end of the sands at a little promontory, natural erosion has created a rocky amphitheatre, a bowl in the rocks known as Cat Pool, and on the rock wall like a cave painting is depicted the life-size figure of a white stag. Above on the highest point of the promontory is the squat, white lighthouse whose round windows and arched doorway create a cute little face. These two features, the stag and the smiley lighthouse, have become local icons, and I sat around for a while and took in the views and the air. I met a delightful gentleman of a certain age like me who turned out to have been born in Cullercoats close to my childhood home in Tynemouth. We lingered and chatted for a good while, and amused ourselves with so many shared memories. It never ceases to amaze me that encounters such as this happen all the time when one sets out, alone, to explore. It's one of the reasons I do this.

Sitting there on my own in the shadow of the great castle and with all this around me I felt a deep wistfulness that I couldn't linger in this place; that I was only passing through.

Cat Pool with the white stag and the lighthouse face – photo: the author

I ambled up the headland where at The Point the view north over Harkness Rocks reveals the enormous panorama that is Budle Bay and the flats of Lindisfarne beyond. I ought to have been able to see the castle on Holy Island but the mist had returned and I couldn't. Never mind, I knew it was there. I could see that on the vast seascape of Budle Sands there was not one solitary soul, no one at all, Northumberland at its best, in the silence almost achingly remote and serene.

If you could do it, it would be a very long walk across Budle Bay, but you can't really get across Budle Water which runs through it. Even the Northumberland Coast Path and St Oswald's Way take a long, long detour inland to bypass the flats and sands here around Lindisfarne. For those so inclined, the intrepid and the determined, it's possible to drive around the inland side of the bay and park at the end of one of the small tracks that run down to the occasional farm near the coastal flats, and then walk for a mile and half or so to the sands that I could see across Budle Bay, before the island of Lindisfarne. These are Ross Back Sands and the long slog on foot to get there is worth every yard. Unspoiled, empty sands and vast views are the rewards. It is uncompromisingly remote here, and standing at the north end of Ross Sands one can imagine being alone in the entire world. I related earlier that Druridge Bay is one of the longest stretches of beach, and it is, but the immense scale of sand here around Lindisfarne trumps it, and anything else, a thousand times. A merely observational description might suggest a bleakness to this place. But it is not bleak, it is majestic.

The empty vastness of Ross Back Sands
Photo: Derek Taylor

At the northern point of Ross Sands is Guile Point, as remote as you can get and where two, tall navigation pillars guide boats into the harbour at Lindisfarne. Across the water is Holy Island itself with its small fortress castle and ruined priory, tantalisingly close, but impossible to get to from here. So I took the car around, keeping to the minor roads closest to the bay. A one way in one way out dead-end track took me to Fenham Flats, a huge nature reserve at the head of Budle Bay. At the end of the track, little more than a place to pull in or turn the car around, a fence gave immediately onto the marshes and sand flats, the squelchy mud and tussocks literally just over the fence and stretching as far as the eye could see to the horizon where the ridge of dunes before Ross Sands and the distinctive navigation pinnacles on the point, standing like matchsticks painted on the skyline. Through these flats run numerous tidal rivulets with wonderful names like Stinking Goat, Cathangings Letch and Foulwork Burn. A heritage board by Natural England tells us, amongst other things, that during autumn and winter the Lindisfarne National Nature Reserve hosts a third of the world's population of East Atlantic Light-bellied Brent geese. However this was summer and I expect the geese were elsewhere. I stood entirely alone looking out over to Lindisfarne and the castle peering gloomily out of the mist. This is unspoiled nature in salt, ozone and a silence broken only by the occasional seabird's cry.

I was forced briefly back onto the A1 for just a few miles before the turn-off at the Lindisfarne Inn, to which I'd return later. The road wanders a mile or so through country hedgerows and fields, crossing the main east coast line then suddenly emerging onto the flat pancake of Holy Island Sands. Caution signs confront the traveller, urging due heed to the numerous tidal warnings. The causeway runs alongside marker poles which guide more intrepid walkers across the flats and past the refuge post, a hut on stilts that provides a sanctuary for those who disregard the tide-times.

Like very many others I parked in the grassy field at the entrance to the village and went off to explore.

The refuge on Holy Island causeway – photo: Nathan Atkinson

The island is more substantial than the casual visitor might imagine. The village itself is big enough to accommodate pubs, a hotel, various shops, a distillery and much in the way of old stone cottages where beguiling side-lanes and alleys abound. There are the ruins of the priory where much history is to be found and where Bede and St Cuthbert collaborated in the beginnings of Christianity in this place. There's a decent harbour where upturned boat-hulls, traditionally converted into little huts, provide colourful features on the shore and then a short walk to the castle, which is more like a keep, standing high on a bluff with line of sight to Bamburgh in the south, and to the walls of Berwick in the north. The island itself allows for decent walks out to its further coastline where ever-more remote sands and flats recede into the distance and the North Sea.

Lindisfarne, or Holy Island, captured in various moods and light

Left – *Photo: Claire Johnson*

Right – *dawn*
Photo: David Thompson

Left – *calm causeway*
Photo: Paul Turner

I had hardly arrived in the village when it came on to rain and I was forced into The Ship Inn. I was released from The Ship when the rain eased off, but unfortunately it came on again just as I was passing The Crown & Anchor. I nosed around the old priory and the shop at Lindisfarne Meade where free tasting sessions and one of the best gift shops I have encountered can delay the traveller.

From Lindisfarne, two of the great castles of Northumbria caught together in a fine juxtaposition - Holy Island in the foreground and Bamburgh beyond. Very different origins, but each serving a similar purpose - defence and security.   *Photo: Paul Turner*

The village was, in fact, really very quiet, which was odd in view of the crowded car park. I wondered where they'd gone but the island is, as I related, more substantial than one might think and can swallow a car park load without much difficulty. After a wander around the harbour and a walk along the shore I was fearful of missing the tide and getting stuck for another 5 hours, so I took myself back to The Lindisfarne Inn to discover what turned out to be another excellent base from which to explore further north. I hoped that the weather would improve because I'd been told that the places I'd encounter are wonderful.

The Lindisfarne Inn at Beale, near Holy Island
Photo: The Inn Collection Group

ELEVEN

LINDISFARNE TO BERWICK

The Northumberland Coast Path approaches Lindisfarne by the same route as both St Cuthbert's Way and St Oswald's Way, but the latter two split away and follow the causeway onto the island. The Coastal Path continues up the coast alongside the sands and dunes surrounding the northern aspect of Holy Island, Goswick Sands. This enormous area of sand, ironed flat by the hand of nature, from Budle Bay in the south, around Lindisfarne and up to here at Goswick Sands is no less than stunning in its vastness, its empty enormity. In most places inaccessible to all but the most determined, it is the sanctuary of coastal wildlife, birds, seals and the host of creatures that make this place their home. This is a wild and desolate place in many ways, but also of undeniable natural beauty, scoured by the wind and swept clean by the tide. There is little evidence of the hand of man here. I would have been more likely to encounter a polar bear than a discarded crisp packet. My presence here was briefly tolerated by me leaving no trace, no memory of my visit.

This horizon-wide breadth of sands gradually returns to Northumberland's traditional pattern of bays and dunes as eventually the expanse of Goswick Sands withdraws and blends seamlessly into Cheswick beach.

The great expanse of Goswick sands, looking south towards Lindisfarne   Photo: the author

Cheswick Beach looking north towards Berwick   Photo: the author

Access to the coastal sands around here is still very limited and pretty impossible by road. Even with good boots and poles walkers need some determination to explore it. I took a long country road, deserted for the most part, through miles of arable land and fields of livestock, surrounded by views of timeless farmland. This took me through narrow lanes to Cheswick, a hamlet where the road divides and the lane to the south led me through the unexpected sophistication of Goswick Golf Club, its car park full of Range Rovers and BMWs, its manicured links busy with diamond pullovers - a surprise to anyone, including me, in the middle of all this empty landscape. Beyond the golf club the lane wanders south towards the coast, the course itself between it and the shoreline. Parking is either impossible or discouraged here, by the golf course on the one hand and by occasional homesteads and farms on the other. At the end of the track, at a farm where I found the gate to be firmly closed, the persistent explorer might find a way to clamber over the dunes onto Goswick sands where the horizon suddenly expands to a beautiful, wide beach and shimmering white surf with views of the castle on Holy Island to the south and the distant structures and iconic pinnacle chimney at Spittal and Berwick to the north. This was my way onto Goswick Sands. Others may make the long hike up the Coast Path from the Lindisfarne causeway to bring them here.

From the village of Cheswick and taking the other route down to the coast, a couple of miles through more farmland and unspoiled countryside I arrived at a steeply hump-backed bridge over the east coast line, a dead end before the dunes of Cheswick beach and a few places where a car may be parked. By the bridge I was moo'd at by huge herd of black cows from over a fence. I declined their attention and made my way through the dunes to emerge onto the white sand of Cheswick beach. On perfect cue the sun came out, delivering striking light and warmth on my face and I sat on a sun-bleached, sea-weathered log in the sands, spellbound by the beauty of the Northumberland coast around me. I sat with my back against a dune and watched a small group of elderly gentleman deeply engaged in a game of sand boules. I studied them lobbing their boules, walking after them slowly with deliberate steps, heads down and hands behind the back, then they paused and peered down intently at the cluster of balls, presumably to determine or argue about the winner. They told me it was an annual ritual performed on this day, every year, whatever the weather. Such eccentricity is to be greatly admired.

*Sand boules
on Cheswick
beach*

*Photo: the
author*

I sat there for a long time. I examined the day. It's difficult to describe the profound sense of peace and space here, the immensity of the horizon, the silence, the wind-chimes of the birds. Perhaps Shelley or Keats or some other romantic could do it justice, but I'm personally at a loss. I love all these beaches, bays and little coves, and as I have related I have always regarded Beadnell as perhaps my favourite, but here, on Cheswick beach in sun and eccentricity, I felt as if I had reached the pinnacle of perfection, that I had discovered my paradise.

I was loath to leave my hollow in the sand beneath my grassy dune, but with effort I dragged myself to my feet and on up Cheswick beach to where the rocky outcrops of Far Skerr and Middle Skerr lead on to Cocklawburn beach. I recovered the car from where I had left it at the hump-back bridge and drove around to Scelmerston, where the lanes took me back down to the Skerrs and I could explore the low cliffs passing one small bay after another. I wandered down to the shore and meandered around the rocks and sands, interspersed with occasional rocky features and coves. The coastline sands at Cocklawburn are pretty and continue north by features with names like *Redshin Cove*, *The Skipper*, *Toppye Knowe* and *Bear's Head*. I wondered at the origins of those names now mostly lost in time, surviving only by myth, tradition and the long-forgotten hands of those who made the old maps on which they are recorded. That day the coast was almost deserted except for a lone ice-cream van parked rather forlornly amidst the dunes above the beach. I went to speak to the driver, a young man who was reading a book and seemed so surprised to have a customer that I bought a cone from him and ate it on an old wooden bench facing out to sea. Then I went to Spittal.

Left –
Cocklawburn beach
Photo: Claire Johnson

Below – *Spittal beach and cliffs*
Photo: Claire Johnson

Spittal, like Seaton Sluice, is not a distasteful place as its name suggests it might be, not by a long chalk. It's the preamble before Berwick and sits on the south bank at the mouth of the river Tweed. There's a small promenade, the first concrete on the coastline since Seahouses so far as I've seen, which says much about the Northumberland coast. Lining the promenade above a pleasant stretch of sand, loosely strewn with brown wrack, there is a small row of ice-cream, coffee and food outlets, and some public conveniences as befits a place that offers the first promenade for many miles, a real car park and which attracts many visitors. I enjoyed having the views from Spittal beach, south to Holy Island, north into the estuary of the river Tweed, and across to the defensive walls of Berwick and the pretty pier with its little red and white lighthouse.

At a table outside the promenade cafe I met one of our photographers, Claire Johnson. As we sat and chatted the café proprietor complained that customers made her too busy, and the sea sparkled blue in the afternoon sun.

I walked around Spittal Point where the low tide exposes the rocky, muddy foreshore around the estuary, and I went to look at the distinctive pinnacle chimney, a relic of long-gone industry, visible from as far away as Lindisfarne and beyond. It's a wide estuary as one might expect of a significant river like the Tweed, and which for so long marked the border between two nations, although it does so no longer.

Spittal beach and the town of Berwick   Photo: Peter Adcock

I took in the upper reaches, the old bridge and the newer crossings for road and rail. Across the river mouth I regarded the solid, rampart walls of Berwick, a place that has changed not only hands and allegiances but countries over the centuries. Once English, once Scottish and now English again since 1746, its wide defensive walls record a history of changing ally, independence and centuries of challenging resilience.

Spittal is a pleasant place to wander around, a mix of natural estuary and human endeavour, the solid promenade with its shops and cafes, the pier across the river, some light industry hanging on along the banks upstream where Spittal subtly blends into Tweedmouth, old cottages in terraces near the shoreline and newer housing on the rising land above.

Spittal beach, the distinctive pinnacle chimney on the left   Photo: Claire Johnson

It's from here that tomorrow I shall cross one of those bridges and make my way around the Berwick coastline and north towards the border. I'm told it's not an easy place to get to, and whether I get that far remains to be seen.

*The bridges of Berwick – **above** The Royal Border Bridge (1850) and **below** The Old Bridge (1624)*
Photos: Keith Hamblin

TWELVE

BERWICK TO THE BORDER

I looked out of the hotel window over my breakfast this morning and noted the weather with disappointment. A grey, overcast sky threatened to spoil what was intended to be my last day here. However, my hopeful beseechings to the weather-Gods were obviously received sympathetically because by the time I'd got back to Berwick the sky had cleared to a translucent blue dotted with white clumps of cloud and a warm sun shone down on the northern reaches of Northumbria.

Yesterday afternoon I looked across the Tweed estuary at the defensive walls of Berwick, and now I stood beneath them on the north shore looking back across at Spittal and further past Cheswick, Goswick and Holy Island on the horizon. The pier road took me up and around the rocky headland above Berwick's *"Little Beach"*, where the coastal route has now become the Berwickshire Coast Path.

It's right to say here that there is some inconsistency, even mystery, in the naming of the beaches and bays at Berwick. For example, the bay I'd just passed and referred to as *"Little Beach"* is described as such on the website of *visitberwick.com*, which you'd think would probably know about such things. However, the O.S. map identifies it as *"Meadow Haven"*, and Google Earth as *"Berwick Beach Front"*. Thebeachguide.co.uk offers simply *"Berwick Beach"*. My Berwick-based photographer Claire tells me that it's known locally as Meadow Haven, comfortably consistent with Ordnance Survey as you might expect from the bible of cartography. And so it goes on. Greenses Harbour is variously Greenses Haven (google, artuk.com) but given Fisherman's Haven by Ordnance Survey. Actually, Fisherman's Haven is on any view quite a different place and I'm tempted to say that for all its revered authority the O.S. map is wrong, but that would be bold indeed. Anyway, I've done my best with the names, but perhaps it doesn't matter much because, whatever it's called, the scenery of Northumberland is no less exceptional.

I took my time past the coastguard lookout station and the manicured links of the Magdalen Fields Golf Course where there is parking and the little clubhouse offers coffee and snacks to the public. I sat there at an outside table in the sun with my maps and an espresso next to the wide grassy areas where visitors ambled about and children scampered around the play area and an ice-cream van.

I walked on and the coast path took me between the cliff and a large caravan park above Greenses Harbour, not really a harbour at all but a pleasant, sandy bay. The coastline here develops a cliffy aspect in contrast to the sands and dunes that have been prevalent throughout much of my journey up Northumberland, perhaps an indication that I'm approaching a Scottish landscape. As a consequence it's not an easy route to walk below the cliffs where the bays are separated by boulder rocks and any attempt to do so is a very difficult, challenging, slow scramble.

Left – Berwick Beach, or Meadow Haven, looking south

Below – Greenses Harbour or Haven with the old harbour wall

Photos: Claire Johnson

The path took me around the caravans, between the cliff and the fence of the holiday park. The park actually looked very pleasant. The vans seemed to be of a

high specification with outside decking from which those with the benefit of facing out over the coast would have an exceptional view. In one, I passed a little girl about 4 or 5 years old playing with her Grandmother on the van's sun-decking. She was playing with a tennis ball, called out and threw the ball over the fence to me, holding up what appeared to be a luminous green, oversized false hand. Not wanting to disappoint her and with an encouraging look from the Gran, I chucked it back, not expecting her to catch it. It turned out that both the ball and the false hand were made of Velcro and the ball stuck to it like a limpet. I said "That's cheating," and the girl looked at me with what seemed to be sympathy and resignation - the way a child looks at an adult who has simply no idea of how the world works.

Greenses Harbour   Photo: the author

The caravan park spreads around the headland and naturally the grassy, clifftop areas are popular with tourists and the bay below is used extensively by those holidaying there, but on my visit even in July in fine weather it could hardly have been called over-crowded. A few families sat around, children played and ran about, and some braved the long climb down to the beach, and eventually back up again.

Past Greenses Harbour the path continues to wind around the caravans for a short while before the park ends above the next cove, Fisherman's Haven, the last properly sandy bay before the border. Further away from Berwick and its caravans the walk seems to go on and on and the coastline becomes even harder to access due to the east coast mainline which runs close by, in places only yards from the clifftop path. The rocky, boulder-strewn flats which lie beneath the cliffs are almost inaccessible and it's deserted down there, save for the seabirds.

The cliff-top path winds along these rocky shores for a long, long way above the rocky slabs and boulders of *Brotherstone's Hole*, *Needles Eye* and *St John's Haven*. Inland of the path here, where the railway line allows, there are only fields where a tractor was mowing golden grass and sheep were lying about in sleepy contentment, and then I arrived at Marshall Meadows Bay, a small holiday park and a steeply-cliffed bay of rocky slabs, the last bay before the border with Scotland and my final destination.

Marshall Meadows Bay and not a soul on the coastline as far as the eye can see
Photo: the author

There's a large farm at Marshall Meadows, an acre of concrete hardstanding and wide, low, steel barns. It also provides, by way of a coded barrier which leads into the caravan park, the only crossing of the main railway line since back in Berwick. I wanted to have the car reasonably to hand once I'd made it to the border, and this seemed an ideal place to park and walk up the remaining half mile or so of cliff path. So I went back, collected the car and approached a farm-person in the acre of unused concrete and enquired if it would be possible to leave the car in some quiet corner for half an hour while I satisfied my ambition to walk up to the border.

The farm-person's mouth turned down, he informed me that it was private land and there was nothing to see at the border anyway, and then he summarily dismissed me from the premises. Despairing that I might have to go all the way back to Berwick and re-trace my steps back up the cliff path, I sat in the car and studied the map a little closer. I discovered that a small driveway next to the farm led to a discreet country hotel. It was currently closed, undergoing refurbishment, and after driving down the narrow driveway I discovered great activity, a host of builders with dump trucks, noisy diggers, orange overalls, hammers and considerable jollity. They seemed to be a mix of Geordies and Scots, and were delighted to allow me a parking space amongst their muddy equipment, and even directed me to the path down to the clifftop, which, as it turned out, took me back through the concrete farm. I was unassailable on foot as it's a public right of way, so as I passed through to the bridge over the railway line I gave a cheery wave to the farmer I had encountered there a little while before. He did not wave back.

The path here at the top of the cliff runs past fields of long, yellow grass and more sheep. It's surprisingly wide and defined and to my surprise it had actually been well mown, and recently too. I felt the heat of the mid-day sun on my forehead and, I regret to say, on the top of my head, evidence of both my age and my failure to wear a hat. It was also deserted and as I approached the border I was entirely alone. Looking back south from where I had come, the bays and coves I had passed on the clifftop path from Berwick presented the most spectacular view, a crenulation of cliffs, bluffs and a sparkling blue sea. I could not see another soul on the whole of the visible coastline.

A surprisingly well-mown path, East Coast trains and the border in sight
Photo: the author

I didn't know what to expect at the border, or even if it was defined at all in view of what the grumpy farmer had told me. The Ordnance Survey map shows only a thin, dotted line and nothing to suggest the obvious significance of this remote, perhaps rather arbitrary, national divide. However, as I approached on the mown path, I could see that there was something in the distance, something that seemed to be mostly blue.

The border is marked by a proper sign at a gate. It's a big sign and a bold statement that exclaims "*Welcome to Scotland*" and "*Failte gu Alba*" over-printed on a striking Saltire, the white on blue St Andrew's cross of Scotland. I took some photos. I had hoped to get one with me in it but there was no one about to help. I attempted to balance my phone on the fence and use the self-timer but it kept falling off and resulted only in pictures of my foot. I walked through the gate into Scotland, and it didn't feel any different. I stood around for a while gazing at the cliffs snaking off into the distance, running uninterrupted towards Eyemouth some 5 miles to the north. It was some of the most beautiful and spectacular scenery I have ever had the privilege to see. The silence was total, broken only when East Coast trains thundered past every now and again.

So that's it. 11 days ago I stood on the headland at Tynemouth where I still think Northumberland's southern border lies, whatever the Council tell us. Now, 11 days later, I stood in the sunshine at the border with Scotland, the northernmost yard of my homeland county. I've seen just about every cove, every bay, every harbour, every stretch of sand and rocky foreshore on this coastline, and it's been wonderful. I can think of few other lifetime experiences that would surpass the simple pleasure of spending 11 days on the coast of this Great Kingdom, Northumberland.

THIRTEEN

EPILOGUE

I found myself unable to discard this place, reluctant to tear myself away, put down my pen and go home. I stood on the cliffs at the Saltire gate and wondered at the intensity of what I was feeling. There was far more to this than making notes for a book, far more than taking photographs. I felt connected with this place, I felt it in my soul. I felt, in fact, quite overwhelmed.

I also had a desperate, panicky feeling that I might forget, not all of it of course but little parts of it, and there was no part of it at all, not even the smallest incident or view, that I wanted to escape from my memory. All these past days I had spent wandering up the coast, enjoying the hospitality of the hotels, the bars, the idiosyncrasies of the people I met on the way, the sun, the rain, the very *Northumbrian-ness* of it all. It was all important and I wanted to remember it all.

So I took myself back to Cheswick Beach where I lay in the sand with my head resting on a dune and I gazed around at the expanse of sand, shimmering in the sun. I watched the surf brilliant white against a navy blue sea, the horizon sharp against the lighter blue of the cloudless sky. I heard the calls of seabirds and the air was salt and sea. I closed my eyes and I thought nothing could be more perfect than this. This is Northumberland.

No caption required

And now the vessel skirts the strand
Of mountainous Northumberland;
Towns, towers, and halls successive rise,
And catch the nuns' delighted eyes.
Monk-Wearmouth soon behind them lay,
And Tynemouth's priory and bay;
They marked, amid her trees, the hall
Of lofty Seaton-Delaval;
They saw the Blythe and Wansbeck floods
Rush to the sea through sounding woods;
They passed the tower of Widdrington,
Mother of many a valiant son;
At Coquet Isle their beads they tell
To the good saint who owned the cell;
Then did the Alne attention claim,
And Warkworth, proud of Percy's name;
And next they crossed themselves to hear
The whitening breakers sound so near.
Where, boiling through the rocks, they roar
On Dunstanborough's caverned shore;
Thy tower, proud Bamborough, marked they there,
King Ida's castle, huge and square,
From its tall rock look grimly down,
And on the swelling ocean frown;
Then from the coast they bore away,
And reached the Holy Island's bay.

Sir Walter Scott
Lindisfarne, the Holy Island (extract)

Photos: **above** Ebb's Nook: the author   **below**: Derek Taylor   **next page**: Alnmouth: David Thompson

The Photographers

in their own words

 **Amanda Fall -** I only recently moved to Northumberland, at the end of January 2020. I have always had an interest in marine wildlife and conservation, and a secret wish to live by the coast one day. In 2019, I won a stay in a holiday cottage at Seahouses and that trip changed my life. I lost my heart to the Northumberland coast. Somehow fate brought me to Kern Cottage, which is right on the coastal path at Howick, and on my very first morning I opened the curtains to see Bottlenose dolphins jumping in the bay below the cottage. As they say, you could not make it up! The amazing coastline where I live, and the wildlife which calls it home, stirred in me a passion to capture it all on film through photography. From the cottage, you can look up the coast and see Dunstanburgh Castle with the Farne Islands in the distance, looking south you can make out Coquet Island. The history contained within the walls of Northumberland's castles adds, for me, a unique sense of belonging which manifested itself in another curious twist of fate - after my holiday in Seahouses, I was amazed to see a painting of Dunstanburgh Castle on a stall at the Street Fair in the village where I was living in Lancashire at the time. I bought the painting which now hangs in my living room. I took it as a sign that my life in Northumberland was meant to be, and moved up the very next spring.

 **Anne Nicholson -** I have lived in the Seahouses/Bamburgh area since the early 1980s, and even though I was born in Birmingham I think of myself as a Northumbrian as I've been here since I was a child. I'm retired now and I find photography a peaceful pursuit that takes me out of myself and everyday life. The beach is 10 minutes' walk from home and it changes from day to day, sometimes from minute to minute as squalls move through and the light changes with the passing hours. Early morning is a special time to go on the beach and watch the sun coming up, very often just for me. In the winter it means I don't have to get up so early and the colours can be breath-taking. I am so lucky to live on the North Northumberland coast and enjoy all its colours & moods.

 **Ant Clark -** For over twenty years I've been engaged in the art of photography, fine tuning my skills and abilities, and drawing on the many experiences of a varied life of travel around the world. Growing up in the UK, I enjoyed capturing the changing faces of family, friends and local Northumberland landscapes. With its diverse landscape, rugged coast and ever-changing weather. Any photographer who has not travelled to or explored the North East coast will be in for a treat, not just for its photographic opportunities but for the people of Northumberland and their exceptional warmth and welcome.

Claire Johnson - I have lived in Berwick upon Tweed for about 13 years, and I work for the NHS as a community occupational therapy assistant. I grew up in landlocked cities and always wanted to live by the sea. When I came to Berwick and realised my dream I found inspiration for photography all around me – in the beautiful coastline and landscapes in Northumberland, which I would say are some of the best in the world.

Claire Marshall - I was born in Birmingham but moved to Blaydon-on-Tyne as a small child. Bamburgh beach holds many childhood memories for me, particularly playing hide and seek in the dunes with my dad. Later in life, I visited Bamburgh and Embleton with my own children, weeks spent camping by the beach. The sight of my children and their friends tumbling down the sand dunes and having the best of times are wonderful memories which fill me with joy. The peace, harmony and spiritual nature of this ever changing landscape continues to draw me back time and time again.

Darren Chapman - I am a chef of nearly 30 years with an eye for detail. I first picked up a camera in 2016 and whilst learning how to use it explored some of the best locations Northumberland has to offer. I can be found on Facebook @darrensphotos where I make regular posts from Northumberland and beyond.

David Thompson - I was born in Wallsend and now live in Morpeth. I am a landscape photographer who is passionate about Northumberland. You are most likely to find me on the wonderful beaches of Bamburgh, Druridge Bay and Amble on a winter's day early in the morning with a howling gale coming from the north east.

Dawn Roberts - I've lived a stone's throw from Tynemouth all my life, as have my family before me as far back as I can remember. My husband and I love nothing more than to pack the car with a picnic, my camera and, weather permitting, our paddle boards and head off to explore parts of the coast we still haven't yet discovered. I love seeing how my pictures turn out and capture what may become a tiny part of history in years to come. I feel very lucky having so many beautiful views and historic places to visit and photograph so close to home, which is definitely where my heart will always be.

Derek Taylor - I was born in Morpeth, and have lived there all my life. Now retired, my interests include photography and videography. I am actively involved in walking groups and am a photography contributor to the Campaign for the Protection of Rural England (Northumberland), Google Maps and Goforawalk.com. I love the Northumberland Coast from its larger resorts to the picturesque little villages and harbours, the wide expanses of unspoiled beaches and majestic castles and the big skies - one minute clear and bright the next dark and angry, the sea calm and tranquil one moment and the next foaming and raging.

Gren Sowerby - I was born on a farm in south-west County Durham and moved to Tynemouth when aged 10. I have spent most of my life here on the Northumberland coast, and I currently live 200 metres from the seafront in Whitley Bay. I have been a photographer for over 40 years and these days I mainly photograph wildlife, nature and seascapes, using both Nikon DSLR and mirrorless systems. Being an outdoor lover, photography plays a big part in this, being able to capture things like crashing waves on my walks. I love the big winter seas our coastline is renowned for.

Helen Cowan - I have lived in Whitley Bay since 2017, although I was born in Lancashire, moving to Manchester then Brighton, before relocating north again. The thing I love most about photographing the coast is that every day creates a different picture, even if you are standing in the same spot. The colours, reflections and power of the waves never cease to amaze me. Early mornings are my favourite time of the day, the feeling of being alone and witnessing nature's daily miracles is breath-taking. I am retired now and I suppose you could describe the coast as "my happy place".

James Lamb - I am an IT Director and amateur photographer who was first introduced to the landscapes of Northumberland by my father and grandparents as a child and I continue to visit the area frequently, staying mostly in Seahouses. Visiting with my wife and children from home in Yorkshire, I particularly enjoy boat trips to the Farne Islands to watch and photograph the puffins feeding their young. When not admiring the landscapes and sea birds, I can be found experimenting with photography techniques in the dunes, capturing the sunset behind Bamburgh castle.

John Fatkin - Originally from Forest Hall to the north of Newcastle, I now live in North Shields. I have been taking photos for around 10 years after witnessing some fantastic skies whilst out dog walking. After running my own business for 20 years I am now retired.

Keith Hamblin - I was born in Berwick upon Tweed and now live in Belford – not far from Bamburgh and Lindisfarne. I have always been a keen photographer - sport, social events, landscapes etc., but living on or near the Northumberland coast all my life I have always been drawn to the sea. The views, sunrises and sunsets are stunning and this stretch of coastline throws up so many options. I have worked as a journalist on local newspapers all my life and photography has always been a hobby. It's a passion, and capturing the spectacular scenery around Northumberland as a whole is a joy. I couldn't ask for a better place to call home.

Lyn Douglas - I am a semi-retired nurse with a great love of the outdoors. I live on the coast just outside Alnmouth, where I have many opportunities to capture the beautiful Northumberland coastline. I took up photography as a hobby around 6 years ago and have since begun to see the area in all its breath-taking glory. I am a keen kayaker and hill-walker but I am very much drawn to the sea, no matter what its state - flat calm or turbulent waves. That's where you will usually find me.

Nathan Atkinson - I have been interested in photography for over twenty years with a focus on the North of England. Of particular interest to me is photographing our gorgeous Northumbrian coastline, where looking out over the waves, no matter what the weather, removes the daily pressures of modern life. Every time and day in Northumberland can be different, from an incoming storm to the sunrise over a flat sea. It is all magical - the wide sweeping beaches, the abundance of castles, the peace and solitude it gives - there are few other locations like this. I have had some of my work published before and it is a privilege to capture all this so that others may enjoy it as well.

Paul Turner - I was born in Newcastle upon Tyne but have lived in Whitley Bay since I was 3 years old, and I am now in my mid-sixties. When my son got married in 2012 I decided to get a better camera for the occasion and my love of photography began. Since then I have photographed sunrises from Berwick to Whitby, travelling in my little camper van. I love the colours, peace and tranquillity of the early morning and now have taken over 20,000 photos of our beautiful coastline

Peter Adcock - In 2020 I cycled from Tynemouth to Edinburgh via Berwick. I always take pictures on my cycling tours to share with others and there were plenty of wonderful photo opportunities to be had, especially on the coast which was stunning. I was born in London, brought up in Southampton and I now live in Bristol but I'll definitely return to the Northumbrian coast, sooner rather than later I hope.

Will Marshall - I am 24 years old and currently living in Gateshead, only a short distance from the Northumberland Coast. Photography is a strong passion of mine outside of my day job, and I consider myself incredibly lucky to have been born and raised in the North East of England. My favourite time to visit the coast is the early mornings, taking advantage of the sunrise light and the undisturbed landscape. The many historical structures, dramatic rock formations and expansive beaches along the coast continue to draw me back with my camera in hand.

AUTHOR'S NOTE

The physical journey was made over the period 4th – 15th July 2021. I did not walk it all from the Tyne to the border. The practicalities of needing to carry laptops, cameras and all sorts of similar paraphernalia, the need to keep my writing equipment dry, have a constant source of power, the constraints of time, advancing age and the draw of a decent bed all prevented that. There are those who have walked it all, and more, and they have my enduring admiration, especially as many have done it for charity. No, I had my car to assist me. But I saw and walked pretty much every bay, harbour, promontory, beach and rocky inlet on the coastline. I don't think there was an inch of the coast I didn't see, appraise and simply gaze at, and in that sense I did what I set out to do – travel and observe the whole coastline of my birth-county, not in bits here and there, but all in one go.

I want to thank those who encouraged and inspired me, particularly the many strangers I met on the way. Without exception, from the lady on the beach at Low Hauxley to the staff of the hotels and inns where I stayed, I received a warm Northumbrian welcome from all those I encountered.

I also want to thank those who have helped me with the writing, corrected my syntax and grammar and pointed me in the right direction. In particular I want to thank my dear American friend Doug Hermann who, yet again, examined my lines with expert eyes and offered invaluable advice, and also my long-suffering wife Gillian whose line-editing duties were discharged with commendable diligence.

I acknowledge with thanks the permission given by Robson Green to reproduce his lines on Northumberland.

Finally but by no means least, I am indebted to the photographers who have contributed and made this book possible. I include those who submitted photographs to me but whose work, for one reason or another, I could not include. I have been astonished at the enthusiasm, the talent and the dedication of all these people.

Most of all I have been deeply moved by the passion for Northumberland so evident in everyone I met – from photographers to bar staff and those I met casually walking the beach. The north east of England is a special place, and I am proud to have been born and bred here. As Robson Green so succinctly but perfectly described it – *This Great Kingdom, Northumberland.*

ABOUT THE AUTHOR

I was born on Tyneside and spent my childhood and adolescent years there surrounded by the business of shipbuilding (my father was a naval architect) and the seaside resort of Whitley Bay. I was educated at Barnard Castle School on the Durham/Yorkshire border, and at De Montford University, Leicester where I gained an Honours degree in law. My career took me to East Anglia where I eventually became a senior partner of a Norfolk law firm.

Outside of writing, I enjoy painting, the fells of the Lake District and the wide landscape of Northumberland, exploring my heritage and reading. I enjoy many genres of writing, from Daniel Defoe to Sebastian Barry, but I am especially drawn to contemporary travel writers such as Michael Palin, Paul Theroux, Pete McCarthy and Bill Bryson.

I am now retired and live in the city of Norwich with my wife and cat.

My mother and father, John and Moreen Wood, on the road above Low Newton with Dunstanburgh Castle on the horizon.

This photograph was taken in about 1970 when we went there to discover the place my 3 x great grandfather was stationed for 20 years between 1826 – 1846 as a Commissioned Boatman in the coastguard service. My adventures and discoveries there, and in many other places throughout the north east, can be found in my book *"In Search of a Northern Soul"*

ALSO BY THE SAME AUTHOR:

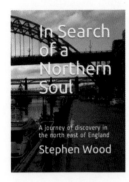

In Search of a Northern Soul – a journey of discovery in the north east of England. (pub. 2020)
A deeply personal but light-hearted and humorous look at the land of the author's birth and heritage. This is an adventure into both the present and the past landscapes of the north east of England, a journey that is light, playful yet often poignant and thought-provoking, exploring the places in which his ancestors lived and worked, looking for their memories and exploring far back in the depths of his own memory for the seeds of their experiences. Not simply a travelogue but heritage, history and beer.

The Cat Who Lives in an Igloo – Discovering Home (pub. 2021)
The Cat Who Lives in an Igloo, Discovering Home, is the first book in the Lulu series. After living on the streets and fending for herself from day to day, Lulu is saved by Animal Rescue and finds herself a comfortable, loving home to live in.

Designed for ages 4 – 8, this is an illustrated story which will engage children and provide entertainment and learning.

Full details, blogs, contact, projects and shop at

www.stephenwoodauthor.wordpress.com/

www.stephenwoodauthor.wordpress.com/

Contact
swoodnorwich@gmail.com
07990 970 980

24, Rose Valley
Norwich NR2 2PX

Orwell House

Printed in Great Britain
by Amazon

21883864R00062